Heretics for Armchair Theologians

Also available in the Armchair Series

Heretics for Armchair Theologians

JUSTO L. AND CATHERINE GUNSALUS GONZÁLEZ

ILLUSTRATIONS BY RON HILL

Westminster John Knox Press
LOUISVILLE • LONDON

Scripture quotations from the New Revised Standard Version of the
Bible are copyright © 1989 by the Division of Christian Education
of the National Council of the Churches of Christ in the U.S.A. and
are used by permission.

Book design by Sharon Adams
Cover design by Jennifer K. Cox
Cover illustration by Ron Hill

First edition
Published by Westminster John Knox Press
Louisville, Kentucky

This book is printed on acid-free paper that meets the American
National Standards Institute Z39.48 standard. ♾

PRINTED IN THE UNITED STATES OF AMERICA

08 09 10 11 12 13 14 15 16 — 10 9 8 7 6 5 4 3 2 1

Library of Congress Cataloging-in-Publication Data

González, Justo L.
    Heretics for armchair theologians / Justo L. and Catherine
Gunsalus González. — 1st ed.
        p. cm. — (Armchair theologians series)
    Includes bibliographical references and index.
    ISBN 978-0-664-23205-4 (alk. paper)
    1. Heresies, Christian—History—Early church, ca. 30–600. 2.
Heretics, Christian—History—Early church, ca. 30–600. 3. Church
history—Primitive and early church, ca. 30–600. I. González,
Catherine Gunsalus. II. Title.

BT1319.G66 2008
273—dc22
                                                    2008013185

Contents

Preface

We have enjoyed writing this book. In particular, we have enjoyed—and been intrigued by—the very notion of "armchair theologians," or of "armchair theology." It certainly means that this is not "office desk" theology. It is not theology for professional or academic theologians—for those of us who enjoy the luxury of long hours sitting at our desks, consulting dozens of books, and then writing something for other theologians to read. It is not—thank God!—theology for other theologians. Indeed, the constant bane of theology through the centuries has been our tendency to think and to write in dialogue with other theologians, with the result that it is often difficult to see how theology affects or reflects the actual lives of believers.

An "armchair" is an interesting sort of place. It may be a place for rest, relaxation, and conversation, but it is not the ideal place for poltroons. This is not "couch" theology, written for "couch potatoes" who are curious about theological issues and who, if their curiosity is not quickly and easily satisfied, will simply push the remote control and go on to something else. In our minds, an armchair is the place where one relaxes after a long day of work; it is the place where one sits across from friends and others and exchanges experiences and opinions about life and about the walk ahead. It is the place where one plans for the next day's work. In a word, it is a place of rest, refreshment, and evaluation along the trek of life. So an armchair theology is a theology for believers taking a respite along the march of faith and obedience. To turn a common phrase around, it is the place where we "talk the walk."

In our case, the task of writing for "armchair theologians" has also left its mark on the way we have worked. What we have written is "laptop," rather than "desktop," theology. If an armchair is a place of rest and reflection along the way, a laptop is the instrument with which we write along the way. A laptop does not really belong in an academic study, nor in an ivory tower. A laptop belongs in airplanes, in parks, in hotel lobbies. When we open it in order to write, we are in the midst of all the walks of life. Even when concentrating on our screen, out of the corner of our eye we see people on their various treks and tasks. It is on a laptop that this book for armchair theologians has been written. It has been written while waiting for a plane, in between meetings, or while attending various church gatherings. It is therefore something like a "laptop theology" for "armchair theologians"—or a theology on the march for fellow marchers. It is our attempt to talk with others with whom we walk. So, fellow walker, as we walk together, let us "talk the walk"!

Justo L. González
Catherine Gunsalus González
Advent 2007

CHAPTER ONE

Why Heretics?

In German, the words for "heretic" and "candle" are rather similar. A colleague of ours studying in Basel discovered this, much to his embarrassment, when he went into a store intending to buy four candles but instead ordered "four heretics." The storekeeper, wishing to be helpful, asked, "What do you want them for?" to which our friend enthusiastically responded, "To burn for Advent"!

Obviously, the humor in the story lies in the shameful and gruesome fact that many heretics were indeed burned at the stake, and that therefore the very word "heretic" immediately brings such events to mind. The image of a heretic in our liberally minded society is someone who is persecuted, tortured, tried, and probably burned for his or her ideas. In other contexts, and from the opposite perspective, "heretic" is practically an insult, meaning one who delights in falsifying doctrine and leading people astray.

But the truth is much more complex than either of these views. Not one of the heretics whose opinions we will study in this book was burned or killed in any other way for his teachings. At worst, some were deposed from positions of importance in the church, and a number were forced to abandon the areas where they had the most followers and influence. Nor were these heretics unbelievers or people seeking to destroy the faith. On the contrary, most—probably all—of them were sincere people trying to understand the Christian faith in their own context, asking important questions from the perspective of faith and seeking to lead others to what they took to be a fuller understanding of the gospel. Finally, even though they and their doctrines were eventually excluded from the mainstream of Christian tradition, they did make an important and lasting contribution to that tradition. As we will see further on, it is largely due to the early heretics, and to the response of the church at large, that we have such cherished treasures as the Apostles' Creed and even the New Testament!

What is a heretic? Put in a nutshell, a heretic is one whose teachings the church at large considers erroneous and even dangerous to the faith. The problem is that, precisely because it is difficult to determine who "the church at large" is, it is equally difficult to determine who is a heretic. There are churches today that hold that anyone who does not believe in creation in six days is a heretic. Others believe that those who do not expect a millennium of peace on earth—or even those who disagree as to whether the millennium will come before or after the return of Jesus—are heretics. In centuries past, the Roman Catholic Church dubbed Luther and Calvin heretics. Luther applied the same epithet to Anabaptists and others.

Calvin had Sebastian Castellio run out of Geneva because he declared the "heretical" notion that the Song of Solomon was a love poem! Later Calvinists declared Arminians heretics. And so the list unfolds, with each church body—and sometimes even diminutive church bodies—proving quite ready to declare that those who disagree with it are heretics.

Were we to follow this definition of heresy, we would have to deal with the entire history of the Christian church—or rather, of all Christian churches and sects, for many of these have their favorite heretics, and many of those heretics are the patron saints of other churches!

Fortunately, our task is much more limited. We will be using a narrower—and therefore more broad-minded—definition of heresy. In the pages that follow we will deal only with a very limited number of heretics, a list determined both by chronological and by theological criteria. Chronologically, our list will be limited to those heretics who lived up to the time of the Fourth Ecumenical Council, which gathered in Chalcedon in 451. Theologically, our list will be limited to those whose views that, from the perspective of the vast majority of Christian leaders then and throughout the ages, threatened the very core of Christian faith.

Along this last line, it is important to remember that there were many disagreements in the early church and that most of these did not go beyond that point. People disagreed, for instance, as to the role of reason and of philosophy in the task of theology. They also disagreed as to the date for the celebration of Easter, the authority of bishops, and many other such matters. Such disagreements often bordered on the ridiculous. For instance, in the fourth century, when Jerome translated the Bible into the common Latin of his time—a version known as the Vulgate—he translated the plant that provided Jonah with

3

shelter as a "gourd." The earlier translation said it was an ivy. (The truth is that nobody, even to this day, knows exactly to what plant the Hebrew word found there refers, though many scholars believe it was a castor bean plant.) Some people were scandalized at the change. They even declared that Jerome preferred a gourd so he would have a place to stash away his drink! For a while, mostly in North Africa, the debate ran high and wild. But even so, neither the "gourdists" nor the "ivyists" were declared heretics. They disagreed among themselves, but their disagreement certainly did not touch the heart of the Christian Gospel.

In brief, the "heretics" discussed in this book are only those whose teachings threatened the faith itself. And even among these, our discussion will be limited to the first five centuries of the Christian church, even though we will certainly point out where some of those ancient heresies still live and how they may still lead us astray as to our understanding of the faith we profess.

There is another way in which we must also correct our understanding of what a heretic is. The common image of a heretic—and one often promoted by the church itself in times past—is that of a willful person intent on promoting error. Nothing could be farther from the truth. Most

heretics were convinced believers, seeking to clarify the full meaning of the faith. They asked questions that needed to be asked, even though their answers were often rejected by their fellow Christians. By the very act of posing such questions and suggesting answers, they helped the church at large clarify its faith. While a few may have been people given to idle speculation, and some others may have been tools of people with ulterior designs, most were people deeply concerned for the truth of their teaching and the faith of the people. Some were popular pastors whose preaching and wisdom were widely admired.

As we begin this rapid survey of "heresy" in the early church, it is important to note that the very notion of "early church" may be misleading. For most of us, a church is an organized body of believers, with established leaders and rules of government and of behavior. Indeed, many of our modern churches have been born out of a disagreement over one or more of these matters, and in that case the new body rapidly defined itself in terms of its own organization, leadership, and doctrines. But the early church was not such an organization. For this reason, many historians prefer to speak of the very early days of

Christianity as "the Jesus movement," and others speak not of "Christianity" but rather of "Christianit*ies*."

As the message of Jesus Christ began spreading, it was understood by different people in different ways. We can see this in the earliest writings of the New Testament, the Epistles of Paul. In Galatians, as well as in Romans and elsewhere, Paul refutes the teachings of those we have come to call "Judaizers." The very fact that Paul had to refute them indicates that they had a significant following, and that Paul himself saw the danger that their teachings would spread and become dominant. When Paul wrote Galatians, the outcome was still in doubt, and the Judaizers had as many misgivings about Paul as he had about them. Paul's correspondence with the Corinthians also shows that in that church there were a variety of opinions, not all in agreement with him. Apparently some believed in life after death but not in the resurrection of the dead. Paul's need to clarify what he took to be the true nature and best use of the gifts of the Spirit is a clear indication that there were also divisions and disagreements on these matters. If some claimed that they were of Apollos, others of Cephas, and so on, each of these groups must have had a different understanding of Christianity, or at least of some aspects of the Christian life. Actually, the variety of Christianities in Corinth was such that there were even some who countenanced incest on the basis of Christian freedom!

There are many other instances illustrating the wide variety of Christianities during the first and early second centuries. We know, for example, that when persecution and war forced the early Christians to leave Jerusalem, a number of them settled in the city of Pella. This community was not led by one of the apostles, as we would expect, but by Jesus' relatives—for which reason it has been dubbed "the Christian caliphate." In Acts 18–19 there are some rather cryptic references to "disciples" whose beliefs were not exactly the same as Paul's, for these disciples had only "the baptism of John [the Baptist]." One of them was Apollos—of Corinthian fame—whom Priscilla and Aquila taught "more exactly the way of Jesus." Acts mentions this—as well as the presence in Ephesus of other folk with beliefs and experiences similar to those of Apollos—almost in passing, but it is a clear indication that there were "disciples" whose Christianity was not exactly what later generations came to understand by that name. There were other Christians who insisted on celibacy for all believers and on strict dietary observations.

Thus, the early Christian movement included many different interpretations of the teachings of Jesus and his significance. To speak of "Christianities" rather than of "Christianity" reminds us that there was no established universal system of authority with the power to decide who was right and who was wrong. Furthermore, during the time we will be considering in the early chapters of this book, the church had no support from the state or from society at large—and often experienced open hostility and persecution. This left no other means to decide what was heresy and what was orthodoxy than to "slug it out" theologically

as well as organizationally—in other words, to debate whose teachings and whose church were true and whose were not. It was only after the church had the support of the state, when the great councils of the fourth and fifth centuries gathered to make decisions about heresy and orthodoxy, that it was possible to decide on these matters on the basis of the decisions of established authority. Even then theological debate was paramount, for often there were still disagreements as to which councils were in fact authoritative and which were not. Increasingly, as we will see in the later chapters of our survey, the state and its power were brought to bear on such matters—with the tragic results of physical punishment for those declared to be heretical. Still, during most of the period we are considering, theological debate was paramount in deciding who was a heretic and who was not.

Another important element in such decisions—one that is often overlooked by theologians as well as by historians of doctrine—was the worship of the church. In the early church, worship influenced theology at least as much as theology influenced worship. Thus, when it came to deciding who was orthodox and who was not, an important factor was whether what one taught reflected the faith that was expressed in worship.

What we now consider orthodox Christianity—what is in the New Testament and in the creeds—is the expression of the faith of those who won, and the understanding of early Christian history that resulted from their own perspective. Hence, there is a common notion that from the beginning the Christian church was a fairly tight organization headed by the apostles, that it was they who went out as missionaries throughout the world, and that it was they who determined the future shape of the church. Yet the New Testament itself should suffice to raise some doubts

about this view. Paul himself went out as a missionary and founded churches without having consulted with the apostles about his mission or being commissioned or authorized by them. This is why his defense of his own apostleship is so necessary: not only was he not one of the Twelve, but he had not even been sent by them! (See Acts 5:1–4, where it is clear that it was the church in Antioch that commissioned Paul and Barnabas, and where their legitimization comes from their having been called and sent by the Holy Spirit.)

The reason for stressing this vast diversity within early Christianity is not to cast doubt on the final outcome of the debates of the time, but rather to help us attain an idea of how crucial and lively those debates were. It was not a matter of an official church casting out those whose teaching it found erroneous, but rather of different positions and perspectives clashing among themselves, some coalescing into what eventually became the Christian church, and others rejected and eventually considered heresies.

It is also important to note that there was one very significant difference between what eventually became known as "the church" and those whom we now know as "heretics." That difference was that, while each heretical group insisted on its own doctrines and views as the only correct ones, the church at large—the incipient Christian church—allowed for a certain diversity of opinions and views within its own ranks. This may be seen in the very list of books that came to form the New Testament. Much has been made in recent times—mostly through the popular media—of those books the church excluded from the Christian canon. What is not often said is, first, that in general of all these books are of much later origin than the Epistles of Paul and the four canonical Gospels. Second, and more important for our argument here, the media seldom acknowledge the obvious fact that the supporters of these

books—writings such as the *Gospel of Truth* of the Valentinians, the recently published *Gospel of Judas*, and many others—never sought to have them included in the canon or list of Christian Scripture. They did not, because they insisted that theirs was *the* true interpretation of events and *the* sole authoritative book. There was no need for a canon or list of inspired books. Theirs was it! In sharp contrast to this attitude, the incipient church—those who eventually won the debates and the struggles of the time—was willing and even eager to include in its list a variety of books that did not always agree among themselves but that generally expressed the beliefs of the church at large. Thus, the one great difference between the heretics and those who eventually came to be known as "the church" was that the latter was willing, within limits, to accommodate a variety of views, while the heretics insisted on their own—whatever that was in each particular case—as the only correct one. It was for this reason that the nascent church began to refer to itself as "catholic." The word itself means "according to the whole," or "according to all." Thus, while the Valentinians had the *Gospel of Truth* and some others had the *Gospel of Thomas* or the *Gospel of Judas*, the "catholic" church proclaimed the Gospel according to Matthew, and according to Mark, and according to Luke, and according to John.

This goes against the common stereotype of the church being narrow-minded in contrast with the open-minded attitude of heretics, when in fact the opposite is closer to the truth: at least in the early centuries of Christianity, it was the heretics who rejected all views but their own, and most often the church at large allowed for more latitude than did the heretics.

In the chapters that follow, we will refer to the church whose general consensus was being formed, and that eventually rejected the teachings of various churches, as the "catholic" church. This was still a church in formation, however, a church seeking to define the limits within which it should be "according to the whole" while retaining the integrity of its message. Indeed, it was the need to define such limits that led the nascent catholic church to declare that some views were unacceptable or heretical.

Since in this book we will limit our attention to the great heresies of the early centuries—those that helped the church clarify the very essence of its message—the heretics discussed here were the ones who raised some of the crucial issues in Christian theology. First, there was the question of the relationship between Jesus and all that went before, particularly in the faith of Israel. Some tended to minimize the newness of Jesus and to see him merely as one more episode in the long history of Jewish tradition. These will occupy our attention in chapter 2. At the other extreme, there were those who claimed that there was no connection between Jesus and Israel. To these we will turn in chapter 4. In between, we must deal with another crucial issue also having to do with the continuity between Jesus and what went on before his birth, although in this case the question was posed regarding the entire physical world. How did Jesus and his message relate to the physical world that existed long before his advent and that still exists? This will be the main issue that will occupy our attention in chapter 3, although not exclusively. A parallel question, to which we will turn in chapter 5, has to do with the newness of the gift of the Spirit. Then in chapter 6, we will see the struggle of many Christians with the question of the relationship between the divine as present in Jesus and the divine as the Father and source of all, as well as the divine Spirit present in the life of the church. Here we will see how this question led to the development of the doctrine of the Trinity and why some positions in this regard were declared to be heretical. In chapters 7 and 8, we will look at two heresies: Donatism, which helped clarify the nature of the church, its sacraments, and its holiness, and Pelagianism, which was concerned with the degree and manner in which salvation comes from God and from God alone. Finally, having discussed the nature of the divinity in Jesus (chapter 6), the church had to deal—as we will in chapter 9—with the question of how Jesus is both human and divine. In chapter 10, we will review and assess the contribution of these ancient heresies: how they helped the church define its faith and its message, and how we still see in today's church the results of those early struggles with heresy.

However, before we move on to the next chapter, one point needs to be stressed once again: the heretics discussed here were not evil people who set out to weaken or destroy the faith. When they proposed what they did, matters

were still in flux. Therefore, in order to understand them, we must make every effort to understand them in that context, not as we often imagine them—as cardboard figures to be shot down—but rather as believers struggling with truth as we all do.

CHAPTER TWO

The Ebionites

As was the case with the names of many other ancient heresies, the term "Ebionite" had a life independent of its origin. In other words, we can look at the group in the second century that was termed "Ebionites" and discuss its features—which we will do. But the term has developed a meaning of its own, so that later groups, even in our own time, that are called "Ebionite" will not have all the features of the original group, but only the central one the church deemed the essential unacceptable element. Nor will there necessarily be any historical connection, any continuing link, between the original and later groups that are so dubbed.

The term "Ebionite" is generally viewed not as based on the name of its founder, as some believed in the early church, but rather on the Aramaic word for "the poor," and is a title they may have applied to themselves. Since all we have are later writings rejecting and refuting their views, it is difficult to know exactly who the Ebionites were, how they originated, or what they taught. People criticizing others often draw caricatures of their enemies, and this may have happened with the Ebionites.

There is no doubt, however, that the Ebionites developed out of Jewish Christianity, perhaps as an offshoot of the Jerusalem church after it moved out of Jerusalem shortly before the destruction of the city by the Romans in 70 CE.

After leaving Jerusalem, several groups of Jewish Christians appear to have developed in relatively independent ways. The major group continued its connection to the larger church that was becoming increasingly Gentile and so is not our concern here. They simply became part of the larger orthodox Christian community. But other groups also developed, with various degrees of connection to Judaism. It was not only Christians who were scattered with the destruction of Jerusalem. Remnants of the Essene community who were also scattered may well have joined some branch of the Jewish Christians who had fled the Romans. (The Essene community near the Dead Sea was destroyed by the Romans in the same campaign that ended in the destruction of Jerusalem. They were the group that left the Dead Sea Scrolls, whose discovery in the late 1940s has given us a far better understanding of the variety of Jewish thought in the first century.) We know that the Essenes referred to themselves as the poor or meek who would inherit the land, a promise made in Psalm 37:11 that may be the source for one of the Beatitudes. If it is true that the Ebionites included among their ranks some former Essenes, it is possible that the influence of the latter may be seen in the very name of the group. So these Jewish Chris-

tians may have been influenced by those who joined their congregations from the Essenes rather than from orthodox Judaism.

What we do know is that the Ebionites were followers of the law, to whose ceremonial injunctions they strictly adhered, and saw Jesus as a new teacher who upheld the law of Moses rather than ending its ceremonial features. The Ebionites kept the Jewish Sabbath as well as the Christian Lord's Day, and they held to circumcision, though it is not clear if they demanded this of Gentile converts to Christianity. They turned to face Jerusalem when they prayed. Evidently they had daily ritual baths as well as the Christian baptism of initiation into the community.

However, while the Ebionites stressed the ceremonial law, they believed that the books of Moses—the Pentateuch—had been radically misinterpreted by traditional Judaism. One such error was in taking the commandments regarding sacrifices as God's final purpose. The Ebionites believed that when the Israelites made and worshiped the golden calf in the desert, God told Moses that they were not ready for true spiritual worship and gave him the law of sacrifices as a lesser and temporary evil.

Jesus came to correct that and institute the true worship of God. In this disapproval of temple worship and sacrifices, as well as in the frequent ritual baths, there are overtones of Essene beliefs.

The Ebionites used some form of the Gospel of Matthew, although they omitted some sections of it—particularly the account of the virgin birth. They also held that Jesus did not eat a sacrificed lamb at the Passover meal, which would have seemed a continuation of the law of sacrifices they rejected. In fact, their opposition may have been not only to animal sacrifices but also to the eating of meat.

The Ebionites began very early, at a time when there was no official New Testament. Most of the writings that even-

tually were collected as the New Testament were already circulating among the churches, but they had not been joined into a single collection. Most churches had some but not all the books that eventually were considered canonical. Among the Christian writings that were then circulating, the Ebionites did not like Paul at all. In fact, they viewed him as an enemy of true Christianity because he not only taught that the ceremonial law of Israel no longer needed to be kept but also stressed that Jesus was the true incarnation of God and not simply a prophet in the line of Moses. Paul saw the death of Jesus as the sacrifice that ended all sacrifices. His death was the ultimate Passover, freeing his followers from sin and death just as the original Passover had freed the Israelites from bondage to Egypt and from the death of the firstborn. Paul wrote, "For our paschal lamb, Christ, has been sacrificed. Therefore let us celebrate the festival" (1 Cor. 5:7–8). The Ebionites would have found this totally unacceptable. They would readily agree that Jesus had ended all sacrifices, but they could not accept the notion that Jesus himself was a sacrifice. They also rejected such views because they made Christ something more than a teacher of the law. However, others from the Jerusalem church—and most Christians elsewhere—would have agreed with Paul on these issues and found the Ebionite view unacceptable.

We know that some forms of Jewish Christianity—that is, congregations made up of Jewish Christians who still kept much of the ceremonial law, including circumcision— continued for several centuries, but only at the edges of the Roman Empire. The rapid growth of Gentile Christianity lessened any impact they might otherwise have had. They seemed to survive by their remoteness, and whatever little increase there was in their numbers was mainly through their own birthrate.

Many in the greater church found the Ebionites' continued use of Jewish ceremonial law unacceptable, and the Ebionites could be among those groups Paul and others refer to as "Judaizers." However, we do not know whether they were interested in Gentile converts—as the "Judaizers" in Paul's Epistles were—even if such converts were willing to keep the law. Perhaps they were agreeable to Gentile congregations not keeping the ceremonial law but felt that Jewish congregations should. This would mean that Jewish and Gentile Christians could not share the same table, an issue that would contradict Paul's statement that in Christ "there is neither Jew nor Gentile."

There were other elements in Ebionism that were unacceptable to orthodox Judaism as well as to orthodox Christianity. Though they believed that God was the only creator and had indeed created this world, the Ebionites included in that creation an evil feminine force along with the good, masculine power. The kingdom of this world is given over to evil by God, whereas the world to come is in the hands of good. Jesus is the ruler of the future world, and those who follow him now will be with him in the final

kingdom. Both good and evil have had numerous manifes-
tations, beginning with Cain and Abel. The law of Israel
was from Moses, who was good, but was corrupted by the
evil principle to include animal sacrifices. John the Baptist
was the evil principle, and Jesus the good.

All of these may seem strange ideas, but they were part
of Ebionism. Yet when the church at large dealt with
Ebionism, the central issue was none of these strange doctrines. In fact, even some of the early writings accepted by
the church contain hints of some of these ideas. What the
church rejected was Ebionite Christology. For the Ebionites, Jesus was the most recent—and even the most powerful—of the long line of instruments of the good. He stood
in the line of Abel, Moses, the prophets, and others, but he
was a human being who was being used by the force of
good. He was born as are others, with no virgin birth, and
he is no true incarnation of God in our midst. He was not
God but rather a vehicle used by God. So from the second
century on, when some were accused of being "Ebionite,"
what this meant was that they believed Jesus to be fully
human, even endowed with divine power, but not God.
Many of these people dubbed "Ebionites" believed that at
the baptism of Jesus an archangel in the form of a dove
entered him and gave him this divine power. The words
"This is my beloved Son" indicated that he was now
empowered by God but still only a human being. In this
sense, Ebionite Christology is the opposite of Docetism,
which we shall encounter in the next chapter.

This view also implies that Jesus was mainly a teacher
and not a redeemer. For the Ebionites, his teaching was a
restoration of the Mosaic law that had been corrupted.

The Ebionites represent a form of very early Jewish
Christianity that accepted Jesus, but only to the extent that
he and his work could be understood within the framework

of the Hebrew Scriptures. Granted, they added many non-scriptural features to that picture, but the role of Jesus was still well within the line of Moses and the prophets, who spoke for God. Within the early church there were other groups that held somewhat similar ideas, all of them offshoots of Jewish Christianity.

Within many of the major cities of the Roman Empire, many Gentiles held the Jewish community in high regard. Jewish monotheism and moral laws were viewed by many non-Jews as admirable. Even in the New Testament we hear of "God-fearers," such as Cornelius (Acts 10)—that is, Gentiles who attended synagogue meetings and agreed with the moral law and monotheism of Judaism but who did not follow the laws on the Sabbath, food, or circumcision and therefore did not become Jews. Jews were viewed more as philosophers, those offering the way to the good life, than as an alternative to the various religious cults. These cults were ways to appease the different gods.

Though clearly Christians did not participate in these religious ceremonies, since that would be considered idolatry, they too were viewed as alternative philosophers, and by the second century there were debates among Greek philosphers, Jews, and Christians, each proposing a different understanding of what the "good life" is and how to live it. In these debates, the frequent charge of Jews against Christians was that they were not monotheists but believed in two gods: the God of Israel, whom they accepted because they used the Hebrew Scriptures, and Jesus.

We have an account of, or the notes for, one such debate between the famous Christian apologist Justin Martyr and Trypho, a Jew, from the middle of the second century. In that writing, Justin acknowledges that there are those who call themselves Christians yet believe that Jesus was only a human being endowed with special powers by God. These would be the Ebionites. What is interesting is that, regardless of all the other characteristics of their teachings, by Justin's time the critical issue in Ebionite teaching, that which the rest of the church found unacceptable, is that Jesus was not viewed as God. Justin himself holds to monotheism and explains that it is the Wisdom, the Logos, the Sophia of God that became truly incarnate in Jesus. This is similar to what we find in the prologue to the Gospel of John. However, Justin made a sharp distinction between "God the Father" and God's Logos or Sophia, whom he even calls a "second god." This would prove not to be totally satisfactory, and it set the stage for later debates and controversies (see chapter 6).

In the third century, a Christology appeared that had overtones of Ebionism, although its origins were different. This movement is often called "adoptionism." The Ebionites could be called adoptionists since in their view the power of God had, in a sense, adopted Jesus. These later

adoptionists, however, were not Jewish Christians. They often lived in areas where traditional Jews were a significant intellectual influence, and these Jews were accusing Christians of having more than one God—the God of Israel and Jesus. In a way, this was a continuation of the debates Justin had faced a century earlier. This posed a serious problem, since for many Greeks it was the monotheism of Christianity that was its main attraction. The most significant proponent of an adoptionist Christology in the third century was Paul of Samosata.

Paul was a civil official who became bishop of Antioch in

the year 260. At that point Antioch was subject to Palmyra, whose queen, Zenobia, supported Paul. This is perhaps the earliest instance of state power intervening in church politics. It occurred in a period of relative peace for the church, between the time of persecutions in the middle of the third century and the outbreak of even greater persecution at the beginning of the fourth century. During this time, some politically well-connected people had been joining the church. Some members of Paul's church were concerned with some of his actions as well as his theology. He did not believe that hymns should be sung to Christ as though he were God. He did believe in the virgin birth, but held that the power of God joined the infant Jesus at conception and that this power of God was not God but rather the same power that had inspired the ancient prophets. It could be a higher degree of such power, but nonetheless, Jesus was not God but a man empowered by God.

The technical term the church has used for this view is "dynamic Monarchianism." The word "dynamic" comes from the Greek word meaning "power," and we use it in words such as "dynamo" and "dynamite." The word "Monarchianism" means only one ruler, as in monarchy, in this case meaning that there is only one God ruling the universe and that God has given power to Jesus. This preserves monotheism, but at the cost of denying the divinity of Christ. (Another form of Monarchianism, called "modalistic Monarchianism," "Modalism," or "Sabellianism," preserved monotheism by holding that God has had three different modes: the Father, who became the Son, who became the Holy Spirit. That did not deny the divinity of Christ, but it presented other problems, as we shall see in chapter 6.)

Although Paul of Samosata's political connections had kept him in power for a while, various local church synods

condemned him, and he was finally deposed when Palmyra became part of the Roman Empire after Emperor Aurelius defeated Zenobia.

Ebionism is the beginning of a sporadic history of attempts to understand Jesus as only a human being, but one who was chosen by God and given power by God. There are great varieties of this idea, and all can be viewed as forms of adoptionism. Some place the adoption of Jesus by God at his conception, as did Paul of Samosata, and accept the virgin birth. Others place his adoption at Jesus's baptism, using the words from heaven as their support. In that case, it was his moral and faithful life up to that point that made God choose Jesus as his adopted Son. In all these cases, the function of the special power given to Jesus was to speak God's Word, thus placing him in the line of Moses and the prophets. He was basically a teacher, but a teacher with a divine word. This opinion enjoyed renewed favor in the Renaissance period, with a form of unitarianism that began in Italy in the sixteenth century. It was known as Socinianism, named after its founders, the uncle and nephew Laelius and Faustus Socinus. Because any public statement opposed to the Trinitarian theology adopted at the Council of Nicaea (which we shall discuss later) was illegal, the Socinians were forced to move outside of the Holy Roman Empire. They settled in the city of Racov, Poland, and there wrote a catechism. This writing was directly related to the development of English Unitarians in the next century. Socinianism and various other unitarian views were opposed not only by the Roman Catholics but also by the newly created Protestant churches.

Wherever rationalism is a strong influence in theology, Ebionite or adoptionist views are likely to appear. This was true with the Socinians, but it was also true in some of the liberal theology that emerged in the nineteenth century. Jesus becomes a teacher of the moral law but in no sense a redeemer. His death shows the depth of his belief, and is an example for us, but is not an atoning action.

For the early church, it was clear that Jesus was somehow God. To deny this was a denial of the means of redemption that the incarnation, the cross, and the resurrection implied. Yet the affirmation of monotheism is as essential to Christianity as it had been to Judaism. How could both of these statements be affirmed? How could Jesus be divine and there still be only one God? It would not be until the fourth century that these questions would be faced directly.

CHAPTER THREE

Gnosticism

The world has always been a difficult place in which to live—and a reality even more difficult to explain. There are wars, oppression, injustice, and all sorts of evil that people perpetrate against one another. But even apart from such obviously human actions, evil seems to permeate the entire world. There are earthquakes, floods, and droughts. There are scorpions and vipers. The law of tooth and fang rules the animal world. Humans seem to be able to survive mostly because their "teeth and fangs" are longer and sharper—or because our minds make it possible for us to rule the animal world, often with greater cruelty than any animal. At the end of it all, even for humans who consider themselves all that powerful and important, there is death and corruption.

This predicament has long puzzled people trying to

make sense of it all. The obvious and in some ways most comforting answer is that evil is somehow connected with physical, material reality, and that even though this world and its matter are evil, there is a good reality beyond—a purely spiritual realm without bodies or death. In that case, the ultimate purpose of life is to flee from its own materiality, and concerns over bodies are to be set aside in order to focus on that ultimate purpose.

At the time of the advent of Christianity, such ideas were fairly popular in the Mediterranean basin. Over three centuries before Christ, Greek philosophers—most notably Plato—had spoken of the existence of two worlds. One is this physical world we see and in which we live, with all its pain, perplexity, and imperfection. The other is a purely spiritual realm of ideas, which are much more real than their representations here on earth that we take for reality. Humans are in fact spiritual beings. Our souls belong in that higher realm. We must not allow our bodies and other physical realities to hide this fact from us, or to make us forget it.

Such notions became quite common in the Hellenistic tradition and were succinctly expressed in the Greek pun *soma sema*—the body is a sepulcher. From their perspective, the body, rather than being good, is an impediment standing in the way to fullness of life.

It was not only the Greeks and their intellectual descendants who held to such views on the nature and value of the physical world and of the body in particular. From the East—Persia and Mesopotamia—came even more radically dualistic notions claiming that there are two eternal principles, good and evil, or light and darkness, and that the problem with this world and this life is that these two principles have mingled, so that there are sparks of goodness and light in this evil and dark world. Such sparks are primarily the human souls, elements of light trapped in the darkness of the body awaiting the day when the barrier between light and darkness will be restored and all souls will live in light. In movements emanating from those Persian traditions, one of the ways to free the soul from the body was to starve the latter. In one particular system, the "perfect" would eventually starve themselves to death, while the "hearers" were allowed to eat only a limited range of foods—one of them being beans, apparently because it was believed that there was a spark of spirit (*pneuma*, which means both "spirit" and "wind") in beans and that by eating them one contributed to the liberation of that spiritual reality! Many other religious and philosophical schools held similar views.

Even though some Jews did embrace this absolutely negative valuation of the world, this was not—and had never been—the typically Hebrew stance. On the contrary, the Hebrew Scriptures begin with a story about God making the world and seeing that it was good. The religion of Israel celebrated God's power over seas and mountains,

over rivers and fields, and even over human history, because the God of Israel, the Almighty, was the Creator and Sustainer of all things.

Then Christianity came into the scene. It soon gained large numbers of Gentile converts. It probably also attracted some elements within Judaism that were not satisfied with the traditional religion of Israel and that saw in Christianity an alternative to that religion. Many of these people shared the common notion that the world and its matter are evil and believed that this view was perfectly compatible with the Christian message.

Foremost among those who held such views were the gnostics. During the early centuries of the Christian era there really was no such thing as an organized or coherent gnostic religion. There were many gnostic schools, each borrowing and reshaping ideas from the other, and often in fiercer competition among themselves than against what came to be known as orthodox Christianity. Today we refer to them as "gnostics" because that was the name some of them took, as well as the name given to them by orthodox Christians who sought to refute and ridicule them. But there were many differences among them, and therefore we also refer to them by the names of their founders (the Valentinians, the Basilideans, etc.) or by the particular doctrines distinguishing them (the Ophidians, the Cainites, etc.).

Like the ancient Sophists, many gnostic teachers were grandiloquent, impressing people and trying to outdo each other with their high-sounding language and mysterious words. Toward the end of the second century, in what appears to be a fair description of their vain eloquence, Clement of Alexandria ridiculed them, saying that they were like old shoes: full of holes but with tongues like new!

In spite of their many disagreements, these various groups had a number of elements in common. First of all,

they all explained the existence of the world not as the result of the will of a good God, as in Judaism and in orthodox Christianity, but as the result of an error or of malice on the part of some celestial being. The result was a dualistic understanding of reality in which there are things, usually all material reality, that are evil, and other things— usually spiritual reality, including human souls—that are good. Poking fun at such teachings, North African theologian Tertullian, writing some twenty years after Clement of Alexandria, comments, "My God made heaven and earth, and you cannot point to a measly vegetable yours has produced over all these centuries!"

In this regard, most of these groups—like Jews and Christians—held that there is only one principle or beginning of all things. In Gnosticism this purely spiritual principle was often called the *pleroma*, or "fullness." Within it there are series of distinct beings, also purely spiritual, which most gnostics called "eons." In each gnostic system there were different numbers of eons, often tied to astronomical observations. For instance, in the system of

Basilides there were 365 eons, each corresponding to a different day of the year. In other systems some eons were given names that in Greek were masculine (Word, Abyss, etc.), and others were given feminine names (Truth, Wisdom, etc.). It was then claimed that pairs of these eons begat other lesser eons, until at the end of this process one of these eons—far removed from the origin by this process of generations—begat the world, mostly as a mistake, or, as some would say, as an "abortion." It is against such teaching that 1 Timothy 1:4 warns its readers "not to occupy themselves with myths and endless genealogies that promote speculations."

As we today read the apparently endless lists of eons and their generations, we find it difficult to understand how such views could have been as attractive as they were for people in the first century. This is partly because, after all, most of what we know of early gnostic teachings has come to us in the works of ancient Christian writers whose purpose was to refute them, and who therefore presented the various gnostic schools—and Gnosticism as a whole—in the most ridiculous light possible. Gnostics certainly explained the origin of the world by means of such generations of eons. But even though their opponents made much of such endless generations, this was not the reason for their attraction.

The main reason for the attraction of Gnosticism was not that it offered an explanation for the origin of this apparently evil material world. Its main attraction was that it promised a means to escape from the world. What Gnosticism promised was nothing less than "salvation"—salvation as an escape for the soul from the material world.

This salvation was the second point that various gnostic teachers held in common. Salvation was usually attained by a secret knowledge—in Greek, *gnosis*, hence the name of the entire movement. In many systems, this knowledge provided the secret key to ascend "through the spheres." This was based on the astronomical views of the time, which saw the earth at the center of the universe, surrounded by a series of spheres—usually seven, corresponding to the sun, the moon, and the five most visible planets. Gnostics held that the *pleroma* lay beyond these spheres, which acted as layers of imprisonment for the soul, precluding its ascent to the *pleroma*. But if upon arriving at each of these spheres the soul knew the secret to pass through it—usually a secret password—it could continue in its ascent, eventually reaching the joy of the *pleroma*.

Third, and perhaps most importantly, gnostics generally

proved quite willing to pick up bits of wisdom from a variety of sources and then to piece them together into their own systems. It was this that gave rise to Christian Gnosticism. There were gnostic systems quite apart from Christianity, or only marginally influenced by it. But as Christianity began its preaching, and gaining adepts, many gnostics began incorporating Christian ideas and names into their systems. Thus, very early in the second century Christian Gnosticism arose. Many in the early church saw this as a greater danger than unadulterated Gnosticism. By including elements of Christianity, this sort of Gnosticism became more attractive to Christians. It therefore threatened to obscure the uniqueness of the Christian message, as well as a number of biblical principles.

The first and most important point at which several gnostic teachers appropriated Christian elements—and certainly the most dangerous from the point of view of orthodox Christians—was the very name and person of Christ. Christians proclaimed that God had been manifested in Jesus of Nazareth. Many gnostics claimed the same thing but gave it a different twist. For them, Jesus was a messenger from above—or from the *pleroma*—who brought to earth the message of salvation, to remind souls of their divine nature, and to provide the secret knowledge necessary for one's return to the *pleroma*.

According to most gnostics, Jesus entrusted the secrets of salvation—the saving *gnosis*—to a favorite among his disciples, and not to the rest of them. All others were "carnal," or "physical," and Jesus did not entrust his secret teachings to them. But the favored disciple, the truly spiritual one, received the liberating and secret *gnosis*. Most Christian gnostic teachers claimed that their secret knowledge had somehow been bequeathed to them by that favored disciple. This may be seen in the famous *Gospel of*

Judas, whose recent publication made quite a splash in the press, although it actually says little that was not known before. There, Judas is the favored disciple, the only one who really understands Jesus' message that the soul is entrapped in the body and must be freed for its ascent into the fullness. This is the reason why Judas "betrays" Jesus—although his action was not really a betrayal but an act of obedience to the Master, who had to be freed from his physical body.

In this regard, Christian gnostics presented a threat to orthodox Christianity not simply because they appropriated the name of Jesus, but particularly because in doing so they actually denied or limited the real humanity of the Savior. If the material world is evil, and if Jesus is the alien messenger from a purely spiritual "beyond," it stands to reason that he did not have a true physical body, as humans do. He simply took on the appearance of a human body thus to communicate his message to those souls which he came to free from bondage to material bodies. Or he took a special kind of body, not made of earthly matter but of a special substance from the spiritual world. This notion that Jesus did not have a real human body is usually called *Docetism*, from a Greek word that means "to appear" or "to seem": Jesus seemed to be a human, with a physical human body, but this was mere appearance. He did not eat; or, if he did, it was not because he needed sustenance, but rather to keep the fiction that he was truly human. Some Docetists claimed that Jesus was not born but simply appeared, so to speak, "out of thin air." Marcion—whom we shall discuss in the next chapter and who was not actually a gnostic but held many points in common with Gnosticism—affirmed that this happened during the reign of Tiberius Caesar. That is, Jesus appeared just in time to begin his public ministry. Gnostics also claimed that Jesus had not really suffered and died on the cross. This sometimes led to wild imagination, as in the case of those who said that along the way to Calvary, when Simon of Cyrene was made to carry the cross, Jesus secretly exchanged places and bodies with him, so that the one who was actually crucified was Simon and not Jesus!

Another such Docetist was gnostic teacher Cerinthus, who claimed that "Jesus" and "Christ" are not the same but are actually two different realities. Christ is the messenger from beyond. Jesus is the phantasmagoric body that Christ took upon entering this evil world. Some interpreters believe that the following words in the First Epistle of John are written to reject notions such as those Cerinthus espoused, particularly his distinction between Jesus and Christ: "Who is the liar but the one who denies that Jesus is the Christ? This is the antichrist" (1 John 2:23). And there is no doubt that the following words are addressing Docetism in general: "Every spirit that confesses that Jesus Christ has come in the flesh is of God, and every spirit that does not confess Jesus is not from God" (1 John 4:2–3).

Second, Christian gnostics undermined the authority of the church at large to teach the gospel. If the true gospel was in fact a secret "spiritual" knowledge entrusted by Jesus to a favored disciple and then passed on to that disciple's followers, what all other Christians taught was at best the public teachings of Jesus—things he said that only the true, secret disciple could understand and that therefore the other disciples, and then Christians in general, understood in a "carnal," unenlightened way.

Finally, Christian Gnosticism generally rejected the ethical teachings of the church at large. If the body is by nature evil and has nothing to do with the soul, which is by nature good, two opposite and extreme consequences may follow. On the one hand, one may come to the conclusion that the task of the true believer is to mortify and punish this evil body, which holds the good soul prisoner. Thus, most gnostics advocated an ethic of asceticism: extreme fasting, sleep deprivation, self-punishment, and absolute celibacy were among the many ascetic practices that some gnostics proposed as ways to help the soul free itself from the body. But on the other hand, out of the same premise that the body is by nature evil and the soul is by nature good, the exact opposite conclusion could be drawn: if

there is no way in which the evil body can do good, and no way in which the good soul can be damaged by the actions of the body, it follows that the actions of the body are of no consequence. This seems to have been the position of some who are usually called "gnostic libertines."

Still, on the question of ethics, no matter whether one was an ascetic or a libertine gnostic, all agreed that, the body being of little consequence, there was no need to be overly concerned for the suffering bodies of others. For this reason, Ignatius of Antioch, one of the most ancient Christian writers rejecting gnostic teachings, reports that the gnostics "do not care for the widow or the orphan" and adds with a touch of irony that those who believe that Jesus is a mere appearance are themselves an appearance. They seem to be Christians but only appear to be so, for they ignore those in need.

Fifth, Christian gnostics tended to withdraw from the worship of the church. This was partly because they believed that other worshipers, being unenlightened, were not true worshipers. But it was also because the center of Christian worship was the Eucharist—a meal. How could the eating of bread and the drinking of wine have anything to do with purely spiritual truth? Are not bread and wine part of this material world, the result either of the malice or of the ignorance of an eon or some inferior being? For that matter, what about water in baptism? How can physical water—water like that which drops from the clouds and flows in the rivers—be connected with the true rebirth of the truly spiritual believer?

Finally, bringing all these things together, one could say that Christian Gnosticism denied or subverted all of orthodox Christian teaching. Indeed, some seem to have delighted in taking Christian Scripture and turning it upside down. The Ophites—from the Greek *ophis*, or "snake"—declared that in the Genesis story it was the serpent who told the truth. The Cainites made Cain their hero. As we shall see in the next chapter, Marcion too—although, again, he was not a gnostic—interpreted the Hebrew Scriptures in exactly the opposite direction from Israel and the church.

Gnosticism died out eventually, although it did not entirely disappear. Throughout the centuries the church has had to struggle with the tendency to consider the physical world evil and to understand salvation as being liberated from this evil body. It has also had to struggle with those who believe that salvation is attained by means of special knowledge—either secret knowledge or, most commonly, a particular detail of doctrine that is necessary for salvation. A pervasive gnostic inclination may be seen in the commonly held notion that Christianity should be concerned only with the soul and not with the body. In the nineteenth century, partly through the influence of New England transcendentalism, the movement known as Christian Science took on many gnostic features. In more recent times, as many people abandon organized religion and seek truth and meaning in ancient esoteric teachings—often teachings that claim to be ancient but are in fact modern inventions—Gnosticism has enjoyed a revival. Perhaps, after all, it was the serpent who spoke the truth! Perhaps the church has lied to us all these years! That such views are attractive to many is part of the reason why so many take *The Da Vinci Code* as fact rather than as a mere work of fiction. Perhaps, were he to return today, Clement of Alexandria would still be amazed that it is so easy to mistake the tongue for the shoe!

But even apart from such strange and wondrous doctrines, Gnosticism did have an impact on Christianity that is still felt throughout the church, for much of what we do

today bears the imprint of the early church's rejection of such doctrines. This is particularly true of two features of church life resulting from the struggle against Gnosticism.

The first of these is the doctrine of apostolic succession. Gnostic teachers claimed that they had received their secret doctrines from an equally secret tradition connecting them with Jesus. In response to such claims, Christian writers during the second and third centuries argued that, if Jesus had any secret teachings—which he did not—he would have entrusted them to those to whom he entrusted the church, namely, the apostles. These in turn would have taught such secrets to those who would succeed them in leadership in the church. Therefore, if one really wishes to know what Jesus taught, one simply has to look at the leadership in those churches founded by the apostles. In Rome, in Antioch, in Jerusalem, in Ephesus there are leaders who can trace their connection back to the apostles themselves.

And they all agree on the basic points of Christian doctrine—not like the gnostics, each of whom has a different, supposedly secret, teaching.

Partly in order to bolster this argument, lists began to be drawn connecting leaders in various cities to the apostles. At first, it was not necessary for each new leader—or bishop—to be able to prove such an apostolic connection. It sufficed to be in agreement with colleagues who could prove such connection. Slowly, however, the emphasis moved from doctrine to the connection itself and thus resulted in the principle of apostolic succession, presently held by many churches, that all bishops and pastors must be able to show such connection for their ministry to be legitimate.

The other point at which we see the impact of the struggle against Gnosticism in the life of the church today is the Apostles' Creed. This most cherished item of Christian tradition which Christians repeat week after week was originally formulated in order to distinguish orthodox Christian teaching from Gnosticism and from others who held similar views, such as Marcion. When, Sunday after Sunday, we say, "I believe in God the Father Almighty, maker of heaven and earth," we are rejecting the notion that the physical world is bad. We are claiming that our God made more than Tertullian's measly vegetable! When we say that Jesus Christ "was born," we are saying that he did not just pop up out of nowhere. When we say that he "suffered under Pontius Pilate, was crucified, dead, and buried," we are declaring that he was not a phantasmagoric, fleshless apparition. When we say that we believe in "the resurrection of the body"—or "of the flesh," as the original form of the creed says—we are declaring that the body, part of God's good creation, is good, and that, though much transformed, it too is destined for salvation.

Would Valentinus, Basilides, and the other gnostic teachers be surprised to see that, eighteen centuries after their time, their memory still wafts over the church whose doctrines they rejected? Would Clement of Alexandria be surprised that the echos of those fatuous shoeless tongues may still be heard? Would Christians today throughout the world be surprised to learn how much they owe to these people who twisted the faith and whom the church refuted and rejected?

CHAPTER FOUR

Marcion

In the first half of the second century, precisely at the point when the church was getting organized and clarifying what it believed, a man appeared who both made life difficult for the church and forced it to make decisions whose results we still accept. His name was Marcion, and he was an interesting and complex theologian. The tradition is that he was born into a Christian family. In fact, it is believed his father was a bishop in Pontus, by the Black Sea, an area that very early had a sizeable Christian population. We do not know the date of his birth, but it was probably around the beginning of the second century. He evidently became a wealthy man, engaged in shipbuilding. Since his father was a bishop, it is most likely he was well acquainted with the teachings of the church that would be considered orthodox.

However, at some point he decided these teachings were wrong. He wanted to sever Christianity from Judaism as much as possible. He lived through one of the last serious uprisings of apocalyptic Jews against Rome. That rebellion was put down with great ferocity by the empire. Since many Romans thought that Christianity was a sect of Judaism—which it had clearly been in the years immediately following the death of Christ—many Christians had been killed along with the Jews. Marcion may have assumed that such persecution would cease if the empire understood that Christianity had nothing whatsoever to do with Judaism.

Whatever his reasons, Marcion followed some of the patterns of the gnostics, but with sufficient difference that he must be considered a separate phenomenon. He began teaching in the area of Asia Minor but eventually went to Rome. In 144, because of his teachings, he was excommunicated from the church there as a heretic. At that point, he began organizing his own ecclesiatical structure, one that bore great resemblance to the growing organization of the catholic or orthodox church. In fact, it may have been the need to counteract his organization that gave impetus to the catholic church's own increasingly centralized structure. He had clergy and sacraments, and in worship he read some of the same writings as the catholic church—though with significant differences, as we will see.

Like the gnostics, Marcion did not believe Jesus came from the god of Israel, nor that he was truly born or that he had a truly human body. According to Marcion, Jesus was from a superior god who had nothing to do with creation and matter. The god of Israel existed, and was indeed responsible for the creation of this world and all material reality. That creation, however, was not a good thing for Marcion, as stated in the previous chapter.

Therefore, like the gnostics, Marcion did not believe the Old Testament should be used by Christians. The Hebrew Scriptures belonged to the Jews. They were truly the word of a god, but not of the right god. Marcion held that Christians should have their own Scripture, completely separate from Judaism.

Marcion also believed that the Christian life involved being as free from material reality as possible. He required celibacy of those who were baptized. Sex was obviously very physical, and it led to the creation of new bodies. Therefore, sex was in the service of the god of Israel and must be avoided. Likewise, Marcion did not think Christians should use wine, even in Communion. It was somehow more material than water. For all of these reasons, it would be easy to classify him as simply another ascetic gnostic.

However, the differences between Marcion and the gnostics are probably even more significant than the likenesses. Unlike the major gnostic groups, Marcion did not claim he was the recipient of a secret tradition handed on by one of the Twelve. He had no scripture unique to his group. In Marcion's teachings there was nothing of the *pleroma*—the levels of divine beings emanating from the Father—that was typical of Gnosticism. There were only two gods: the god of Israel, who was not good, and the good, high God from whom Jesus came. Though Marcion held to the conflict between matter and spirit that these two gods represented, he also held to a very different conflict: the conflict between law and gospel, which can also be stated as a conflict between God's justice and God's love.

For Marcion, the god of Israel, described in the Old Testament and Judaism, is a god who gives laws and demands obedience, a god of wrath toward those who disobey. The god of Jesus is forgiving and loving. In Marcion's mind, these two cannot be the same. The god who

GOOD GOD, BAD GOD

gives laws cannot forgive disobedience in regard to them. The god of Israel punishes those who disobey and demands that all of the law be kept. The god of Jesus is graceful; he loves and does not judge and punish. Forgiveness with him is plentiful. These are such contrary characteristics that they cannot belong to the same divine being.

The conflict between spirit and matter does have something to do with love and justice. Much of the law deals with physical reality, with harm to bodies, with physical property. If this physical reality is ultimately irrelevant, the law would be as well. But Marcion's concern goes beyond this connection. It has to do with the nature of love and of justice. The church must answer the question: How do we understand God's love in such a way that the law is not alien to love but part of it? Can the same God give the law and forgive its breaking, without seeming to make sin a minor matter? This conflict between justice and love, between giving the law and forgiving its transgression, between God as lawgiver and God as gracious, is at the heart of Marcion's difference both with the other gnostic groups and with the church catholic.

Marcion recognized that the Christian writings circulating in the church did contain teachings that stressed judgment and law. He therefore created his own canon, his own list of books that should be the scriptures of his church. He was the first to do so. He believed that Paul had the best understanding of Jesus' message, and he therefore used Paul's letters. He included ten letters of Paul (but not the Pastorals, that is, 1 and 2 Timothy and Titus) and the Gospel of Luke, which was the most Pauline. Even these writings he believed had been corrupted by "Judaizing" additions, so he removed all that sounded like law and judgment, all that linked Jesus to Israel. What remained was Paul's contrast between law and gospel, and the grace that Jesus brought. But taken out of context, even those passages now appeared more extreme than Paul's original message had been.

The church opposed Marcion's teachings for several reasons. First, he rejected monotheism, holding to two gods. Second, he rejected the notion that creation and matter were good. The church held that matter, physical reality, is not evil. Sex is part of that good creation and the intention of God. The church opposed extreme asceticism, including mandatory celibacy. The one and only God created only good. Sin has warped this good creation, but it has not destroyed its goodness. In fact, God's redemption in Christ is a redemption of all of creation, not just spirits. What is promised is a new creation, a redeemed world. In these matters, the church's answer to Marcion was the same as to the various gnostic groups. But here also, Marcion differed from the gnostics. Marcion denied the birth of Jesus and his true humanity. But he did believe the crucifixion was essential. He held that Jesus possessed a body of "uncreated flesh" that suffered on the cross. His death was the payment to the creator god for the release of humanity from that god's power. This payment was made on behalf of humanity by Jesus who came from the god of love, who by this action made redemption possible. The catholic church held that redemption depended upon the true humanity of Jesus, a humanity that had the same, created flesh that we possess.

In regard to the relationship of love and justice, the church held that Marcion had seriously misread the Old Testament. It is filled with words of love and forgiveness as well as words of law and judgment. Human beings often sentimentalize love. But parents know that in the raising of

a child, the child must learn lessons about living with others, sharing, and respecting parents and playmates. Those are lessons in law and justice. The child who does not learn this will find life difficult later on. Parents who only try to be friends and never discipline are creating a difficult adult. On the other hand, parents who only make demands and never make allowances for the fact that theirs is a child who is learning, and who punish every infraction harshly, are creating an equally difficult adult. We sense the truth of this connection between love and justice, between making demands and forgiving failures, on the level of human parenting. There is a "tough love" that makes sense, although most of us err either on the side of "tough" or on the side of "love."

Even in the second century, this parental imagery was used by Irenaeus, a major theologian and a leader in the orthodox or catholic church, and it has frequently been used since. God is like a parent, creating the whole human race and not only a small family. Throughout the history of humanity, God is training us, using both love and justice, both law and grace, to help us develop into a mature humanity, one that can live together and with the rest of creation in peace and harmony. The calling of Abraham and the creation of Israel were part of this plan, and the sending of Jesus another step in it, albeit the central one. The church understands this plan of God for the redemption of the world and is called to proclaim it. Therefore, both Israel and the church are the creation of the same God, along with both the Old and New Testaments.

In regard to the conflict with Marcion, Irenaeus wrote:

> For [the God of Jesus Christ] is good, and merciful, and patient, and saves those who should be saved. Goodness does not desert him as he acts in justice,

nor is his wisdom lessened; for he saves those whom he should save, and judges those worthy of judgment. God does not show himself unmercifully just; for his goodness is doubtlessly before judgment and takes precedence. (In *The Ante-Nicene Fathers,* ed. Alexander Roberts and James Donaldson, vol. 1 [repr. Peabody, MA: Hendrickson, 1994], 459.)

The church's problem with Marcion was not only his misreading of the Hebrew Scriptures: they disagreed on the central issue of the interpretation of the gospel.

Throughout the Christian writings there is a call for growth in holiness, for sanctification. Jesus does not abandon the moral law of Israel but helps us to grow into people who are more able to live by it. Paul constantly called the early congregations to lives of greater obedience. He announced judgment for those who paid no attention to the demands of the Christian life. The Old Testament is filled with both law and gospel, as is the New.

Because Marcion had formed a canon—a list of writings deemed "scripture" for the church—which differed from the books that the church catholic was using, the church now began creating its own canon. Probably this would have happened eventually, but Marcion was the goad for the process and may have increased the church's attention to Paul. By the end of the second century, the basic shape of the Christian Scriptures was complete. It included the Hebrew Scriptures, the four Gospels and Acts, and the letters of Paul—including the Pastorals. There were a few popular writings some churches included that later were considered too late in origin to classify as Scripture but are still read as important early Christian writings. It took a bit longer for other decisions to be made about including some of the smaller books toward the end of our present New Testament.

When Marcion was excommunicated by the greater church, he formed his own ecclesiastical structure that lasted long after his death. For many in the Greco-Roman world, Marcion represented a compromise between the catholic church and the gnostics, whose view of salvation included long series of passwords to be learned and a whole spectrum of divine figures. Marcion's Christianity included more familiar elements, such as sacraments and church structure and readings. It was tempting, therefore, for those Romans who had never been particularly attracted by

Judaism to join a Christian body that eliminated all Jewish elements from its teachings. Marcionism, therefore, was a viable alternative and a serious threat to the church. Marcion's churches were sufficiently similar to the catholic church that catholic bishops warned their members to be sure that congregations they entered away from home were truly catholic and not Marcionite. There were still some Marcionite churches in the time of Augustine, late in the fourth century. Evidently, at least at that time, they used the Trinitarian formula in baptism, since Augustine accepted Marcionite transfers into the catholic church without new baptism—which was the generally accepted practice in the case of people who had been baptized in the name of the Trinity, no matter by whom.

Though Marcion was quickly rejected by the church catholic, the question of the relationship between God's judgment and God's grace of forgiveness has puzzled Christians in every generation. There were Christians shortly after Marcion's time who agreed with the church that the God of Israel and of Jesus Christ were one and the same, but held that forgiveness of past sins came at baptism and thereafter the law must be kept if one is to be saved. They believed there was at most only one later forgiveness, which involved a painful process of confession before the whole congregation and years of penance with suspension of admission to the Lord's Supper. Tertullian, whom we met in the previous chapter, held this. He believed that baptism should be given only to adults, preferably of advanced age, since it was a shame to waste the one forgiveness on infants who would probably sin later in their lives. Baptism was like a pardon from the governor of the universe. It forgave all sin before that time. But like an official pardon in civil life, one can hardly expect more pardons thereafter. Tertullian, and those who agreed with him, believed that the law-giving God did forgive, but only once, or twice at the most. God's love was shown in that forgiveness and in the sending of Jesus that

made it possible. At the same time, Tertullian wrote a great deal against Marcion, raising questions about how he could use even water in his sacraments, since water was the creation of the God of Israel whom he rejected.

The early church, particularly in the West, had difficulties with sins after baptism. How good do we have to be? If we say that sin doesn't really matter, then we are denying the stress on sanctification, the growth in goodness expected of Christians. Some divided sins into serious ones that could not be forgiven after baptism, and small ones that could. The church ultimately rejected Tertullian's view that there was only one time of forgiveness possible, but it did so by instituting a whole penitential system, with confession to a priest required. Such confession put one back to baptismal purity. This was the sacrament of penance, usually called "confession," that began in the Western church in the early medieval period as a means of making forgiveness more available throughout the Christian's life, rather than limited to the moment of baptism.

As long as the church was a persecuted minority in the Roman Empire, those who joined were committed and enthusiastic about the new life they were embracing. They formed tightly knit small communities and depended upon one another for support and friendship. They knew that the life of the Christian community was different from life in the wider society of the Roman Empire. In fact, they had not been baptized until it was clear they had made a break with that other life. But when the church became very popular—especially after the early fourth century when it began to be supported by the emperor—the majority of the population wanted to join, partly because it was the thing to do. Many had no intention of changing their lives to live by the standards the church held to, and the church was in no position to refuse entrance to the many who wished to join. Those who had joined earlier now felt the church was "soft on sin" and regretted the lack of law and judgment they now found in the catholic church. Some formed their own groups. Others believed this new "softness" was a necessary and loving thing to do. The church had to be more forgiving precisely because of its new role in society. It now had the opportunity to influence the whole culture, but that would take time and patience.

Often in the church's history the conflict between a God who makes demands and a God who forgives has been raised to the Godhead itself, as a conflict within the Trinity. God the Father is seen as the lawgiver who demands punishment for those who sin, while God the Son is the one who offers to pay the price for humanity in order to meet the Father's requirement of justice. Scripture does not see things in terms of such a conflict, but this has been a rather simple way for Christians to understand how the same God can be both the giver of law and the forgiver of sin. However, such a difference in character of the Father and the Son does great damage to the understanding of the Trinity as one God with a single purpose. It does not solve the problem but rather raises it to an even higher level.

During the Reformation period, the relationship of law and forgiveness was again part of the whole mix of theological issues discussed. The Roman Catholic Church held to the penitential system, which included confession to a priest. Protestants disagreed with this but had a variety of views. Some among the Radical Reformation—the so-called Anabaptists—agreed with Tertullian that sin should end with baptism, and any serious infraction of the law after that involved a long process of confession to the congregation and a time of exclusion.

Luther and Calvin, leaders of the Lutheran and

Reformed traditions respectively, had some significant differences on the issue of love and justice, usually seen in terms of the relationship between law and gospel. For Luther, there was significant contrast between the law, whose major function is to show us our sin, and the gospel, which brings us the word of forgiveness. For Calvin, the giving of the law to Israel was in itself an act of grace, a means of guidance for the people. The major function of the law is to show God's people what they are free to become, the direction in which they need to grow. The gospel is the grace of forgiveness that gives us this freedom. Luther saw more discontinuity than Calvin between the Old and New Testaments.

In the nineteenth century, some Christian theologians could not imagine that Jesus had any connection with Judaism. They claimed that Jesus was not really Jewish. They found little use for the Old Testament in the church, or at least gave it far less authority than the New. Their concern was not so much with the conflict between love and justice as with the ceremonial and dietary laws of Judaism. They found these at odds with the spirit of rationalism—the spirit of the Enlightenment—that dominated the time. Their reasons were somewhat different from Marcion's, though the result was similar. Some decades later the Nazi regime required that the state church teach that Jesus was not a Jew, and we know the terrible consequences of that anti-Semitism. In reaction, in recent decades there has been much more emphasis on the Jewish character of Jesus and the continuity between the Old and New Testaments.

No one in the church wants to be called a Marcionite. Yet remnants of Marcion constantly tempt the church. This occurs in several ways. First, many Christians still today have difficulty combining God's law and judgment with God's grace and forgiveness. Because there is also a widespread lack of biblical knowledge, they fall into simplistic views. The most common is that the God of the Old Testament is the Lawgiver and Judge, whereas Jesus is loving and forgiving. Parents or Sunday school teachers trying to explain to a child the importance of Christmas often tell the child that before Jesus, Jews believed that they had to fulfill the law in order to be saved. Jesus came to tell the world that God is forgiving. What that implies is that God's grace and love were unknown in Israel. That is exactly what Marcion was saying.

Second, some pastors rarely preach from the Old Testament. When a lesson from the Hebrew Scriptures is used, it often appears as a foil for the New Testament reading. That is, the sermon proceeds to show that Israel misunderstood what God wanted. For instance, Israel had animal sacrifices whereas Christians know that God does not want that. But the question needs to be asked: Were animal sacrifices a true direction from God to Israel, or had the Jews mistaken the revelation? Christians do not have such sacrifices. Is that because we now understand God better? Or did God want the animal sacrifices in Israel in order to point to the one sacrifice of Christ that was to come? Is the Old Testament truly the Word of God for us, or is it filled with misunderstandings that the New Testament corrects?

Marcionism is a constant danger to the church. Easy answers to the relation of law and gospel lead to bad theology, and yet many do not want to do the hard thinking and Bible study that will lead to true understanding. There are differences between the Old Testament and the New. But there is also enormous continuity. God has been working since the beginning to bring redemption to a fallen creation. God works throughout history, changing the means but not the goals, just as parents work differently with a toddler than with a teenager.

Even so, Marcion did teach much to the church. From him the church learned the need for a canon of New Testament Scripture—not one correcting or undoing the Old Testament but rather complementing and completing it. In the very need to counteract Marcion's own

church, the church at large gained greater appreciation for the importance of organization and means of governance. But above all, the church's reaction to his views has helped us understand more fully that in God love and justice are not opposed—that God's highest form of love is justice, and that God's highest justice is absolute and unconditional love.

CHAPTER FIVE

The Montanists

Will the real Montanists please stand up? There have been—and still are—many different interpretations of the Montanists. Were they an early women's rights group? A form of monasticism? A strange group waiting for the end of the world? An early Pentecostal group? They were a bit of all of these, but none of them completely.

The movement started when a man named Montanus began preaching and gathered a following. He was from Phrygia, an area near the Black Sea in what is today Turkey. He was originally a pagan priest but had recently become a convert to Christianity by the time he began his movement. In 177, he was excommunicated by the church in Phrygia. There were two female prophets with him, Maximilla and Priscilla, which showed that he gave women an important role in his work. He believed that with his preaching, the new age of the Holy Spirit had dawned, that the Holy Spirit dwelt in himself bodily. This meant that the end of the world was at hand, and the New Jerusalem would descend from heaven in Phrygia, in a small village called Papuza.

Montanus claimed that first there had been the age of the Father, but with the birth of Christ the age of the Son began. Now the third age, the final one, has arrived. The law of Moses was given for the first age. The second instituted the law of Christ, which was even more demanding. Now, in the age of the Spirit, an even stricter law has been given. This meant that the Montanists generally exhibited the works of charity that were characteristic of early Christianity, as well as keeping the faith in the face of persecution. They formed communities in which celibacy was urged. Second marriages were strictly prohibited. There were martyrs among the Montanists, which was not true of the gnostics. Moreover, the Montanists apparently had "spontaneous" martyrs, who volunteered and purposely sought out martyrdom. The wider church did not approve of this. To be a martyr was a calling from God. One should not seek to be one. If one could avoid being arrested or charged with being a Christian without being false to the faith, that was the course to be chosen.

The message of the Montanists was not at all gnostic. The stress on celibacy was because the end was at hand, not because of any rejection of material reality. Montanus agreed with much of the church's teaching, especially about who Jesus was and his relation to the God of Israel. But there was a great deal about the catholic church that he did reject, particularly its growing organization.

We have seen in previous chapters that in the face of the

gnostic threat and Marcion the church had begun to draw up its canon. The books it considered Scripture needed to be as old as possible, preferably dating from the time of the original apostles. The church believed that new, normative revelation ended with Jesus and the events surrounding his death and resurrection. The writings that were closest to that time were therefore the most trustworthy. Newer writings from the heretical gnostic groups were rejected, and even orthodox later writings were generally not included in the canon, though they were considered good for Christians to read. Montanus believed that the Holy Spirit was still revealing new truth, through him and through others, and that therefore the canon should not be closed. There were instances of speaking in tongues as part of the new prophecies.

Support for the movement appeared in Rome and went from there to Carthage in Roman North Africa. There the Montanist message took significant root in the West. It is this Western form of Montanism that we shall emphasize, even though it may not be the original. In the West, there was little emphasis on new prophecy, which had been so important in the East, but the stricter law was appealing to many. The most famous convert to Montanism in the West was Tertullian. He became sympathetic to the Montanist movement in about 206 and finally joined it in 212. We have already encountered Tertullian in his attacks on Marcion and the gnostics. He was also influential in his understanding of the Trinity. He was an extremely important writer in the West, the first to write theological treatises in Latin, and the source of much very solid theology on the issues mentioned. However, he was much more rigid in his moral stance than many others in the church at that time. It was for this reason that Montanism appealed to him. In about 208 he wrote a treatise "On Fasting," in which he justified the strict Montanist fasts in opposition to the more lax practices of the catholic church. In that essay he wrote:

> It is on this account that the New Prophecies are rejected: not that Montanus and Priscilla and Maximilla preach another God, nor that they disjoin Jesus Christ (from God), nor that they overturn any particular rule of faith or hope, but that they plainly teach more fasting than marrying. (In *The Ante-Nicene Fathers*, ed. Alexander Roberts and James Donaldson, vol. 4 [repr. Peabody, MA: Hendrickson, 1994], 102.)

His view was that the catholic church was far too lenient regarding marriage, much more so than the Montanists,

and also much too lax on fasting, but that on actual issues of theology there was no disagreement. This was true in the West, where the issue of the imminent arrival of the New Jerusalem or the direct connection of the Holy Spirit and Montanus were not emphasized. In Tertullian's catholic days he had nothing good to say about women, but he seemed to tolerate women in leadership among the Montanists.

We have seen that in response to the various threats it faced, the catholic church had begun developing a strong structure. This hinged on bishops who, though elected by all the baptized Christians in a city (always all Christians in a city were considered one church, though they might meet most of the time in separate house churches), had to submit a statement of faith to neighboring bishops. If this statement was accepted, then these bishops gathered to consecrate the new bishop. Through this method, both local election and wider approval were guaranteed. If the statement of faith was not considered orthodox, for instance, then the community could elect another. Thus, gnostic or other heretical theologies could be weeded out before their adherents had positions of leadership.

The Montanists did not like this increasingly tight structure. To some degree this was a cultural clash, one we will find frequently in this early period. The great characteristic of Roman civilization was Roman law. This established positions in civil society that had authority and power. The person who held the position had the use of this power, but it was granted by the position itself. Other societies were not so structured. In them, a person held power only because of personal strength or cunning. If a chief or king became physically weak by age or illness, stronger members of the society would wrest power away. In Roman society, however, as long as individuals held a position, they had the power associated with that position, no matter how physically weak or strong they were. (Obviously, coups were always possible, and they did occur, but that was a not a lawful way to do things.)

Within the church, this had important consequences. The church was not concerned with physical power, but spiritual power was another matter. Holiness—clear, manifested holy behavior—was a reason for power in the church's life. This is often called "charismatic" leadership. But as the Roman idea of structure was used more and more in the church, the conflict between two kinds of power became more obvious. If a bishop was elected because he had a relatively high social position—and this was frequently the case, because literacy and education were needed for a religious group whose authority was

written Scripture—that person might be less obviously holy than some other members who had shown their holiness in persecution. A non-Roman congregation might prefer the charismatic authority of the holy person rather than that of the elected one. Tertullian, in "On Fasting," wrote: "Who, among you [catholic Christians], is superior in holiness, except him who is more frequent in banqueting, more sumptuous in catering, more learned in cups? . . . If the prophets were pleasing to *such*, my (prophets) were not" (chap. 17).

This concern for holiness had another dimension for the Montanists. Like many other Christians, they believed the catholic church, with some of its bishops permitting forgiveness fairly easily, was becoming too lenient, too "soft on sin." The Montanists were more demanding in their moral lives. Their message of holy living and the present reality of the Holy Spirit was very attractive to many Christians, especially in North Africa. It was the Montanists'

strictness that they liked, since they felt that the larger church was losing its original moral standards.

Montanism developed and spread in the West partly because of the institutionalization of the church itself. This conflict between charismatic and institutional authority is something that happens in all movements, if they last long enough. Movements usually begin with charismatic leadership, with personalities that embody the message of the group. This was clear with the original disciples, whose message of Jesus and the significance of his death and resurrection won so many converts. At the beginning, there was room for some flexibility in the way congregations developed and exactly what they believed. Paul's letters and Acts both show that there were women prophets and organizers. But eventually—for the church, in the second century—there was the danger of too much diversity, so that the central message of the church could be lost. What the gnostics and Marcion taught simply was not compatible with the gospel as the earlier church had known it. This led to the development of structures and approved teachings that would weed out the conflicting ones. This institutionalization meant the elimination of more charismatic leadership in favor of those whose teachings were certain. In the process, the leadership of women was eliminated. When specific positions are created, and persons have authority because of the office, then it is much easier to say that only men will be appointed, or no one younger than thirty, or other specific requirements that charismatic leadership did not impose.

In addition, as the membership grew, especially when more socially prominent people joined, it was more difficult to keep the same strict lifestyle that was there earlier, when people generally from the fringes of society were overwhelmed with joy to be part of a new family, a new creation. The well-to-do had much more invested in the present creation and therefore tended not to be willing to part with its ways completely.

As all of these things were happening in the church, the Montanists represented a desire to turn back the clock, to have charismatic leadership, strict moral standards, new revelations, allowing more room for the present working of the Holy Spirit. They may have had an idealized view of the earlier church, however. Their stricter standards were made more possible by the expectation of the end of the world in a brief span of time—brief enough that less institutionalizing would be necessary. In the West, it was the stricter moral standards that had the greatest appeal, as well as leadership that showed holiness rather than meeting other requirements. The catholic church never considered the Montanists to be the great threat that the gnostics and Marcion were. The Montanists separated from the catholic church, but the two still had much in common.

Theologically, Irenaeus wrote against them. He upheld

very strongly the closing of the canon, arguing that the highest revelation had been given in Jesus Christ, and thereafter we are dependent on the writings that came from the earliest communities of faith that knew best what had happened. The Holy Spirit is needed to help us understand these writings fully, but there are to be no new revelations that alter these earliest ones. In addition, Irenaeus said that the age of the Spirit had begun at the resurrection and Pentecost, when the risen Christ had sent the Spirit. The new age had not waited until the appearance of Montanus but rather had begun with the birth of the church.

The church opposed the Montanist stress on celibacy. It also allowed second marriages for those who were widowed. Even Paul, who had recommended to the Corinthians that those who were not married might remain so, had based this on the nearness of the end, the expectation of

the return of Christ in the near future (1 Cor. 7:25–40). As we have seen in the conflict with Marcion, the church did not believe that Christ or the Holy Spirit had imposed a law on believers so strict that the work of grace and forgiveness was overshadowed. The Spirit helps us become holy, but this is a process of growth toward that goal rather than a constant measure of perfection.

In addition, an attempt to impose strict moral standards often provokes one schism after another. In Tertullian's case, he joined the Montanists because they were stricter than the catholic church. However, later in the third century there was a group called the "Tertullianists." It may well be that eventually Tertullian found the Montanists too lax and began a stricter group.

We know that Montanism continued in the Eastern area of the church (in rural areas in present-day Turkey) until the sixth century, when it was still opposed by the state, which was now catholic Christian. The last adherents in the East burned themselves in their churches rather than surrender their communities. Montanism had disappeared in the urban areas much earlier. It is difficult to maintain a movement based on the imminent end of the world when the date keeps changing after the earlier ones fail.

In the West, where Montanism was not as apocalytic as it was in the East, the Montanists eventually negotiated a return to the catholic church. This was after the catholic church became the religion of the Roman Empire. This was accomplished fairly easily. Their only request was that their martyrs—those who had died in the great persecutions—should be considered true martyrs by the catholic church and listed as such in the prayers. This meant that the catholic church recognized that these Montanists had died because of their faith, which was a faith the catholic church believed to be truly Christian.

It is possible to see Montanism as an early sort of Pentecostalism, though there is also much difference between the two movements. There was also within the Montanist movement more of a role for women than the catholic church was permitting at that time. At least in the East, there was an expectation of the end of the world very soon, so the Montanists had some similarity to the Adventism and other similar movements that developed in the nineteenth century. Since they formed ascetic communities, they could be thought of as somewhat monastic. But in reality, they were not any of these. They were—especially in the West—a charismatic movement that eventually became known for its strict lifestyle, in opposition to a church that was finding its way as a permanent institution in the world.

The Montanists were forerunners of some later movements that divided history into different ages, with specific characteristics for each age. Montanus held that there were

three successive ages—that of the Father, the Son, and the Spirit—with increasingly strict laws. Joachim of Fiore, in the late twelfth and early thirteenth centuries, held that the Age of the Father was the period of the Old Testament, characterized by law and fear. The Age of the Son began with the incarnation, a time of faith and grace. The third, the Age of the Spirit, characterized by love, was in the process of dawning in his day, showing that the end of history was near. A more complex system, called "dispensationalism," developed in the nineteenth and early twentieth centuries. It was made popular by Cyrus Scofield. In *The Scofield Reference Bible* he divided history into seven "dispensations."

Against all of these movements, the wider church has generally held that the only new age began at the resurrection and Pentecost and will continue until the return of

Christ, the timing of which is known only to God. As Christians, we live in that new time, with one foot in the old creation and one in the new, awaiting the full manifestation of God's rule, for which we pray daily.

CHAPTER SIX

The Trinity

The story, although probably not true, is still worth telling. It is said that a candidate for ministry, appearing before presbytery, was asked about the doctrine of the Trinity.

"Well," the candidate said, "The Father . . . [mumble, mumble]. The Son . . . [mumble]. And the Holy Spirit . . . [mumble]. The three . . . [mumble, mumble] one."

"Would you please repeat that?" asked one of the commissioners.

"Certainly, sir. The Father . . . [mumble, mumble]. The Son . . . [mumble]. And the Holy Spirit . . . [mumble]. The three . . . [mumble, mumble] one."

"I still can't understand you!"

"You are not supposed to, sir. It is a mystery!"

Although probably just a legend, this story is closer to truth than it sounds. Most of us mumble something about the doctrine of the Trinity. We know we are supposed to believe it, and that somehow it is an important element of Christian faith. But we really cannot make heads or tails of it, and we would much rather just mention it and move along to something else.

The Trinity is indeed a mystery. But mystery has beauty and power only as we seek to penetrate it, as we see its far-reaching implications, as it overpowers and engulfs us.

Therefore, it is important that we understand as much as we can of the doctrine of the Trinity—although not so much to explain it as to allow its depth and its beauty to inspire us. In order to do this, it helps to learn something about the heretics against whom it was formulated. Here again, we will find that people who were eventually declared heretics—and usually with good reason—not only were for the most part sincere Christians but also contributed significantly to the formulation of what would become orthodox Christian doctrine. In other words, understanding the heresies against which the doctrine of the Trinity was formulated will result in greater appreciation for the doctrine itself.

In this regard, the first thing to remember is that, in the matter of the Trinity probably more than in any other case, worship came before doctrine. Today we look back at history, and by focusing on doctrine and its verbal formulation, the Trinity seems as much mumbo jumbo as were the words of that candidate coming before presbytery. But this is not how things actually developed, for the church was worshiping God as Trinity long before the doctrine was developed, even long before the word "Trinity" was coined early in the second half of the second century.

All one has to do is look at the earliest Christian docu-

THE USUAL SUSPECTS

ments we have, the Epistles of Paul, to see that this was the case. Paul never sought to explain the Trinity, but he constantly referred to it. In what is probably the earliest of his extant letters—and therefore also the earliest Christian document—Paul refers to "God our Father," to "the Lord Jesus Christ," and to "the Holy Spirit." From his usage of these, it is clear that he considers them as distinct and yet as divine. (The title "Lord," which he gives to Jesus, was the name used for God in the Greek version of the Hebrew Scriptures Paul used.) The same is true of the rest of the New Testament, although different authors express it in different terms. By the beginning of the second century, a Roman official inquiring as to the nature of Christian worship reported that they gathered "to sing hymns to Christ as to God."

Apparently what Paul had to say about the Father, the Lord Jesus, and the Spirit did not cause great stir or concern among believers, for we know of many issues and controversies Paul had to face, but none had to do with this matter. The reason for this is simply that what Paul was saying reflected what the church was doing in its worship. Quite often it would pray to the Father in the name of Jesus, making it clear that the two are not the same. But then it would pray to Jesus and give him divine praise, also making it clear that he is God. The church also prayed for the presence of the Spirit at its gatherings and in the life of believers, and clearly this meant they were praying for the presence and action of God. But, even so, this Spirit for whose presence they prayed and by whose guidance they also prayed is distinct from God the Father and from Christ. We also know that early on the church began baptizing "in the name of the Father, the Son, and the Holy Spirit," as it was instructed to do in Matthew 28:19. Actually, this is the reason why the Creed, originally formulated as questions to be posed to people to be baptized as a way for them to affirm their faith, is structured in three main clauses, each dealing with one of the persons of the Trinity: "I believe in God the Father . . . and in Jesus Christ his only Son, our Lord. . . . I believe in the Holy Spirit."

It was toward the end of the second century that Christians began asking how this could be. The easiest answer was to say that in creation and in the Old Testament God was Father, that God then became Son in the New Testament, and that now, in the life of the church, God has become Spirit. Thus, God appears as Father, Son, or Holy Spirit according to different times and circumstances, much as an actor in a classical play would wear a different mask for each particular role in the play. (This position was sometimes named "Modalism," because God was said to appear in different modes or faces, sometimes "Monarchianism," because it insisted on the oneness of God above all else, and sometimes "Sabellianism," after one of its proponents named Sabellius.)

While this solution seemed attractive, upon closer exam-
ination there were many difficulties with it: Does it mean
that the presence of God in the Spirit is such that when
God is present as Spirit the Father and the Son do not actually exist? Does it mean that when the church receives the
Spirit divine action becomes circumscribed to the church?
What about the many passages in the New Testament
where Jesus speaks of "the Father" as distinct from himself,
or where he promises "another comforter" (the Spirit)?

This view was proposed in Rome by a certain Praxeas, of
whom little else is known. When asked how this could be,
Praxeas simply responded that for God all things are possible. If God so wills, God can first be Father, then Son, and
then Holy Spirit. To this Tertullian, the North African theologian we have already quoted for his wit and mordant
humor, as well as for his adherence to Montanism, declared

that God certainly has the power to do all things. For instance, God could have made a better world than the present one. God could have made a world without vultures. God could even have made a world without Praxeas. But in fact God did not. Thus, to argue about what God could be or could not be makes no sense. The debate is not about what God could do or could choose to be; it is about what God does and who God is.

What most disturbed the majority of Christians about what Praxeas proposed was that it seemed to imply that God the Father, the source of all being, was crucified on Calvary. For this reason, this doctrine was soon dubbed "Patripassionism," meaning that the Father suffered the passion. On this point again Tertullian, that eminently quotable early Christian writer, had something memorable to say. He disliked Praxeas not only because of his Patripassionism but also because Tertullian had become a Montanist (see chapter 5), and Praxeas rejected much of the emphasis on the supernatural gifts of the Spirit that characterized Montanism. Therefore, Tertullian declared that upon arriving at Rome, Praxeas "crucified the Father and put the Spirit to flight."

Tertullian himself tried to clarify the matter with an analogy taken from Roman legal practice; probably Tertullian himself was a lawyer. Quite often in the Roman Empire an emperor shared power with his son, declaring him co-emperor. In such cases the empire itself was not divided. Each had full imperial authority over all the land. Each was fully an emperor, for each was in full possession of imperial power, and that power was not divided. Yet each was not the other. Likewise, Tertullian says, the divinity is shared by the Father, the Son, and the Holy Spirit. There is only one divinity, only one God, just as there is only one empire. And just as the emperor and his son are both fully emperors without creating more than one empire, the Father, the Son, and the Holy Spirit are fully divine without this resulting in more than one God. This led Tertullian to speak of God as three "persons"—Father, Son, and Holy Spirit—and one "substance" of which the three partake in such a way that each has its fullness.

Obviously, many objections could have been raised to Tertullian's proposal, and the value of his analogy could easily be questioned. But apparently Tertullian's explanation raised no eyebrows. This was so because most in the church were content with worshiping the one God, Father, Son, and Holy Spirit, without having to explain how the three could be one. They rejected Praxeas's views and all forms of Modalism, but in general the matter remained there, without arousing great controversy, even though various Christian thinkers expressed different ways to understand the Trinity.

In the fourth century things changed. Constantine, the powerful ruler who had put an end to chaos and internal divisions within the Roman Empire, favored Christianity,

and it seemed that he himself had become—or was about to become—a Christian. Persecution had ended. Converts were beginning to flock to the churches. Preaching, which until then had usually been addressed to the faithful gathered for the celebration of Communion, became an increasingly public event. Eloquent and popular preachers were highly prized.

One of these popular preachers, Arius, became the focus of a debate that eventually provided the occasion for the official formulation of Trinitarian doctrine. In a gathering of the clergy of Alexandria, the question was asked, "Is the Son eternal, as is the Father?" Alexander, the bishop, said yes. Arius said no. What was being discussed was not whether the One who became incarnate in Jesus existed before the incarnation. On this point all were in agreement. The question was rather whether this One existed from all eternity. While this may seem an idle question, it had great significance for Christian faith and worship. If the One incarnate in Jesus is not eternal, this is tantamount to saying that he is not fully divine. And this in turn means that the church has to choose between not worshiping him—though it had done so through the centuries—and confessing that it was worshiping someone who is not truly divine.

The debate grew bitter. Arius insisted on his position. Alexander finally excommunicated him. But then the conflict spilled out into the thousands of Christians in Alexandria. Many of these had been converted recently, after Constantine put an end to persecution and made Christianity socially acceptable. They had not received the instruction that had been customary in earlier times, when the church was not quite as successful. Arius was a popular preacher. How dare the bishop excommunicate him? Someone, perhaps Arius himself, composed ditties that the populace took up and chanted in the streets in protest against Alexander's actions. The scene was probably much like our present-day demonstrations for and against abortion or immigration. People marched on the streets waving placards and chanting, "There was when [he] was not," meaning that eternity existed before the Son. Arius wrote to some of his schoolmates who had studied with him under the famous teacher Lucian of Antioch. He addressed them as "co-Lucianists" and declared that Alexander's teachings were an affront to them and to Lucian, of blessed memory.

Soon the commotion was such that the emperor thought it advisable to intervene. He sent Bishop Hosius of Cordova, his most trusted adviser on religious matters, as a mediator. But Hosius reported that there was no way to reconcile the conflicting views. Constantine had hoped that the church would be "the cement" holding his empire together, much as emperor worship had served in earlier times. And now the church itself was breaking apart. There were also other matters to be decided by the church at large, matters such as how people who had denied the faith in times of persecution should be disciplined and for how long, and issues of church government. Why not hold a great council of bishops from all over the world?

This great gathering took place in the city of Nicaea— across the Bosporus from Constantinople—in 325 CE. Over three hundred bishops gathered. Most of them came from the Eastern portion of the empire, but there were also some from the West and even some from beyond the imperial borders. Although later Christians have seen the Council of Nicaea—eventually known as the First Ecumenical Council—as a theological landmark marking the beginning of the definition of the doctrine of the Trinity, probably what most impressed the bishops present was the gathering

itself and the new conditions it reflected. The church recently persecuted was now gathering at imperial behest and expense. People who had been tortured now sat in a council with the emperor. We are told that one of them, Bishop Paphnutius, from the interior of Egypt, had lost an eye in the hands of his torturers and now bishops came to kiss his empty eye socket.

Since Arius was not a bishop, he was not part of the council, but he had a number of able representatives among his "co-Lucianists." When the time came to debate the conflict between Arius and Alexander, one of the leading "co-Lucianists," Bishop Eusebius of Nicomedia—who apparently was related to the emperor—explained their position quite clearly, apparently thinking that it was eminently rational. But the assembly reacted negatively. They had not been worshiping a creature! They would not worship a creature! Such doctrine must be stopped before it spread any further. At that point, the Arian cause was lost.

After much discussion as to how to make it clear that the church at large rejected the teachings of Arius, it was decided to formulate a creed that would do so. After all, the crucial issue was one of worship: In addressing Christ, is the church worshiping God, or falling into idolatry? The result was a creed to be used thereafter by all churches in their worship. Essentially—with some relatively minor changes made at later times—this is what we now call the Nicene Creed and often repeat in church. This creed clearly rejects Arianism, insisting on the equality between the Father and the Son: "We believe in one God, the Father, the Almighty. . . . We believe in one Lord, Jesus Christ, the only Son of God, eternally begotten of the Father, God from God, Light from Light, true God from true God, begotten, not made, of one Being with the Father. . . . We believe in the Holy Spirit, the Lord, the giver of life. . . ."

All seemed settled until the bishops returned home and were asked how what they had declared differed from Patripassionism. A long debate ensued. The focal point of contention was the word *homoousios*, declaring that the Son is "of the same substance" as the Father. The unity that Constantine had sought was nowhere to be found. Constantine and his successors began having second thoughts about what had been declared at Nicaea, with the result that Arianism gained the upper hand for a while. Among theologians, different parties emerged. The real Arians insisted that the Son is "unlike" the Father. More conciliatory—and perhaps more politically savvy—spirits were content with declaring that they were "like" each other. A growing number subscribed to the suggestion that the Son is "of a similar substance" to the Father. Since in Greek this was expressed in the word *homoiousios*, later historians have quipped that the church was divided over an iota—the letter *I* in Greek. But for people at the time—and not just theologians—it was a crucial issue, so much so that Bishop Gregory of Nazianzen complained that he could not go to the cobbler's shop to get his shoes fixed without becoming involved in a discussion as to whether the Son is *homoousios* or *homoiousios*.

Slowly a consensus was built. Several of the best theologians of the time went beyond easy formulas and cliches into their actual meaning. Foremost among these was Athanasius, the bishop of Alexandria, who had been present at Nicaea as a young man as part of Alexander's staff. Athanasius made it clear that the question was not whether one subscribed to one formula or another. The formula *homoousios*—which he favored—was correct as long as one did not erase all distinction between Father and Son, but *homoiousios* was acceptable, as long as one did not turn the Son into a creature. Along these lines, he insisted that we cannot owe our salvation—our re-creation—to a lesser being than the one to whom we owe our creation. In his view, the incarnation was like the visit of a king to a village. After that visit, the village is never the same. In Jesus Christ, God has visited our human village, and humankind will never again be the same. But this is only true if the one visiting our village was truly, as the Creed of Nicaea said, "God from God" and "Light from Light."

By then the issue had become further complicated because some declared themselves willing to agree that the Son is God but that the Holy Spirit is not. Their opponents gave them the pejorative name of "Pneumatomachians"— enemies of the Spirit.

Finally, in another great council gathering in Constantinople in 381, the decisions of Nicaea were reaffirmed. Now, after the clarifications of Athanasius and others, people found them more acceptable, and they prevailed. By then, it was clear that the church was affirming the full divinity not only of the Father and the Son but also of the Spirit. Thus, one could say that at that point the Trinity finally became the official doctrine of the church. By then, Tertullian's old formula had become standard: God is one substance in three persons.

Since then there has been much discussion on the Trinity. Arianism itself enjoyed a revival when some of the Germanic tribes from the north, who had adopted Arian Christianity during the earlier stages of the controversy, invaded Western Europe. Spain and Italy were under Arian rule for a time. But eventually those Arians were converted to catholic Christianity. At other times Christians have debated various points of Trinitarian doctrine. The worst of these debates was probably the one that took place beginning in the ninth century around the word *filioque*— "and the Son"—which Western Christians had interpolated

into the Nicene Creed, thus stating that the Holy Spirit proceeds from the Father *and the Son*. The rather subtle issues debated need not detain us here. Suffice it to say that this one word still divides the Eastern Orthodox churches from their Western counterparts—Catholics as well as Protestants. During the time of the Reformation, some groups rejected the doctrine of the Trinity, mostly on the grounds that it was irrational. Later, in New England, similar concerns led to the birth of Unitarianism. In more recent times, probably the most significant revival of Arian-like doctrines is to be found in the Jehovah's Witnesses, who claim that the Son is inferior to the Father and a lesser being than the Supreme God.

What are we to make of all this today? First of all, we must try to understand why the debates in the fourth century were so gripping that people discussed these issues in a cobbler's shop and that emperors took sides. What was at stake in the debate that was so important? Aside from the obvious theological considerations already mentioned—for instance, whether Christ and the Holy Spirit are worthy of worship—these matters had practical and social implications that are difficult for us today to see and understand. In the entire Arian controversy, for instance, two conflicting worldviews were expressed. On the one hand, the Arians proposed a God far above human frailty—a God who, like the emperor, sat on a throne high and lifted up, distant from the sufferings and aspirations of the common people. The opposite view declared that the eternal and supreme God was present in Jesus of Nazareth, a Jewish worker executed as a criminal by the imperial authorities. When the church worshiped, it was claiming that God is best known to us in such a Jewish worker. Peasants, slaves, and laborers were worshiping one like them. They were clearly indicating that this Jewish carpenter, humble and poor as he was, stood far above the highest emperor. No wonder then that people discussed these matters in the cobbler's shop! And no wonder that, beginning with Constantine himself and for almost half a century, the majority of the emperors and their immediate staff favored Arianism over the Nicene doctrine of the Trinity.

A word needs to be said regarding the masculine language of the traditional Trinitarian formula: "Father, Son, and Holy Spirit." The debates of the fourth century had nothing to do with God's gender. Indeed, the second person of the Trinity was often called not only "Son" but also "Word" (*logos*, which is a masculine term) and "Wisdom" (*sophia*, which is feminine). The great cathedral of Hagia Sophia, or Saint Sophia, in Constantinople, was not dedicated to a female saint by that name but to the second person of the Trinity. The reason why the terminology of

Father and Son was preferred seems to have been that it spoke of relationships in a way that other less personal terminology would not. In more recent times, as we have become increasingly aware of issues of gender, other terminologies have been proposed. One such suggestion is "Creator, Redeemer, and Sustainer." This formula, while avoiding gender-specific language, has the disadvantage that it seems to bypass the inner relations within the Trinity. (It also has the disadvantage that it is not translatable with the same effect, for in many languages—particularly Romance languages—all three terms are masculine.) Another formula that merits consideration is "Source, Word, and Holy Spirit," although this too sounds rather impersonal.

Finally, these inner relationships within the Trinity have become particularly important in the last few decades as theologians have begun to recover a long forgotten tradition of seeing the Trinity as a model for life in community. From this perspective, what the Trinity teaches us is that true oneness and true glory—the oneness and glory of God—does not consist in standing alone in solitary splendor. It is, rather, a matter of interrelationship. God is one, God is one in a higher fashion than anything else is one, and yet God is one in community. Thus, to those who say that the doctrine of the Trinity asks us to believe in the nonsensical notion that three can be one, we may answer that, on the contrary, the Trinity is a unique example of what it means truly to be one. God's oneness is such that there is love even within the Godhead itself. God is love, not just in the sense that God loves us, but also in the sense that the inner life of the Trinity is a life of love.

CHAPTER SEVEN

The Donatists

The response of the church to the next two heresies—those of the Donatists and the Pelagians—is enormously dependent upon the work of one man, St. Augustine, bishop of Hippo. Augustine is one of the most famous of all the theologians in the history of the Western church, and his influence continues in both Roman Catholicism and Protestantism. The fact that his work is far more influential in the Western half of the church than in the Eastern is also important, for his theology marks a very clear line of demarcation on several central issues—a line that also continues to this day.

Augustine was born in the Roman area of North Africa

in the year 354. His father was Roman and did not become a Christian until close to his death. His mother, Monica, whose name may be a sign of Berber descent, was a devout Christian. Augustine himself did not become part of the church until well into adulthood.

His intellect was obvious very early, and so others sponsored his education when his family could not afford to do so. He became a teacher of rhetoric in Carthage and later in Milan. At the urging of his mother, who had joined him in Milan after the death of her husband, Augustine listened to the sermons of Bishop Ambrose and was converted and baptized. He returned to North Africa and was soon elected bishop of Hippo, a small town near Carthage.

Before becoming a Christian, Augustine had attended meetings of Manicheans, followers of a Persian dualistic religion. He had also studied Neoplatonism, and that had influenced his thought. After his conversion, he wrote refutations of Manicheism as well as Arianism. In fact, his writings serve as a compendium of all of the heresies and movements troubling the church in his own day.

Among his writings are those he aimed at the Donatists and the Pelagians. Part of the reason these are so important is Augustine's ability to discern what is at stake in the various heresies of his day. He was able to show biblically and theologically the essentials that mattered in the various controversies, and he wove together a coherent perspective that protected what was important. While other writers may be more significant in terms of Arianism, no other is as important as Augustine in regard to Donatism and Pelagianism. In these, he had both the first and the last words in terms of the church's response—although, as we shall see, the response to Pelagianism took some interesting turns after his death. Augustine's word was the first because he actually wrote at the time these groups were developing, and his

writings against them led to their condemnation. He had the last word, partly for historical reasons. At the time of his death in 430, the western half of the Roman Empire was disintegrating rapidly due to the invasions of various Germanic groups. The destruction that resulted meant that for almost the next seven hundred years there were few if any educational institutions or libraries that could produce theologians approaching his stature.

This is not to say he was always correct. In fact, his theology, while it definitely protected some things that are essential to the gospel, sometimes led to other problems in the church's teachings. It is always possible to overcorrect the errors of others, and, in some ways, that this may well have been the case with Augustine in both his anti-Donatist and anti-Pelagian writings.

Since soon after its foundation, the church had suffered significant persecutions by the Roman Empire. Those early persecutions were sporadic and local. However, by the third century the church, though still very small, had membership all around the Mediterranean Sea and was increasingly viewed as a threat to the unity of the empire. Serious, empirewide persecutions began early in the third century, lasting for less than a decade. Later, in the middle of the century, there were demands that everyone worship a statue of the emperor, Again, this lasted on and off for about a decade. The most serious persecution broke out in the beginning of the fourth century and was ended abruptly in 313 by Constantine as he gained control of most of the empire. Though Constantine was not baptized until his deathbed, he immediately began supporting the church in various ways.

After each of the major persecutions, the church had to face the issue of what to do about those Christians who had succumbed to the pressure and actually sacrificed to the statue of the emperor, or worshiped other gods, denied Christ, or surrendered the Scriptures or other religiously significant possessions of the church. These were acts the church considered idolatry or blasphemy and viewed as major sins. Some believed that such persons could be reconciled to the church after a period of penance. Others, however, believed that they could never be part of the church again.

After the fourth-century persecution had ended, there was an election for bishop in the city of Carthage. After the election, in the usual pattern, other bishops in the area joined to consecrate this new bishop. No questions were raised about the person elected to be bishop of Carthage, but some people said that one of the consecrating bishops was unworthy to carry out such a function because when the Roman troops had demanded Christian books, he had turned over some, and therefore he was a *traditore*, that is, one who had handed over something he should not have. (It is interesting that our English words "traitor" and "tradition" both come from this same root. In the one case, someone hands over state secrets. In the other case, someone hands on the teachings of a group.) Therefore, they said, the new bishop of Carthage was not a true bishop because his consecration was flawed by an unworthy participant. We have already seen in the chapter on Montanism that there was often a conflict between the Roman view of the power of office and the non-Roman view of the power of holiness. That is the conflict that was being played out here. There was also a serious question as to whether the accused bishop had actually given holy books, or since the troops that asked for them were illiterate he had given them books that had nothing to do with the church. The general Donatist response was that it did not matter. He should have refused to give anything and taken the consequences.

The situation was further complicated by the social and economic setting of Roman North Africa. Much of what today is Algeria and Tunisia was then a colony of Rome and was directly governed from Rome. There were three main population groups in that area of North Africa: the Berbers, who were the original inhabitants of the land, generally lived in small villages in the upper plains; the Punic-speaking population was descended from ancient

Phoenician pirates and settlers and lived mostly in the coastal areas; and the Romans, who had conquered the land and were its most recent arrivals, lived mostly in the fertile coastal areas but ruled the entire region. There were many great estates owned by Romans but worked by the local, non-Roman population—many as slaves. These estates produced much of the wheat and olive oil needed by Rome. The leadership of the church itself was largely Roman, and the language of the church was therefore Latin. There was resentment on the part of the Berbers, both in the church and in society at large, about Roman control. It was the Berbers who held to the demand for holiness rather than simply elected office as a source of authority within the church, and the case of the consecration of the Carthaginian bishop was the spark that began a strong movement within the church.

After the protests had begun, a man named Donatus took charge of the movement, and it took its name from him. He was called "Donatus the Great" and was the leader from 313 on, though the split in the church continued long after his death. The Donatist church preached generally in Berber. This does not mean that there were no Romans among the Donatists or non-Romans among the Catholic Christians, but the ethnic lines were very significant.

The Donatists claimed that any church that recognized the newly consecrated bishop of Carthage was also a fallen church. Since churches in the East and even some in the West that were far away from North Africa had little idea what the Donatists were saying and readily recognized the new bishop of Carthage, this meant that for the Donatists the true church was only their own group in North Africa.

Later in the century some more radical groups associated themselves with the Donatists, though their connections are not clear. These were violent groups that wanted

to kill the Roman landlords. Within the church itself some Donatist groups forcibly rebaptized people and insisted that they remain part of the Donatist churches. In some areas of Roman North Africa the Donatists were stronger than their rivals, and persecution of the latter was a reality.

By the time the Donatists were a strong group in North Africa, Constantine had become the sole emperor and was supporting the church. Constantine and most of his successors viewed the church as a unifying force for the empire and did not want divisions. We saw that in the Arian dispute. The state therefore viewed the division of the church in North Africa as negative, and the question of state intervention to put down the Donatists became a serious issue.

There are several issues that Augustine raised in this context. The first is not about the Donatists themselves but about the state's response. Even though Augustine's episcopal see was not a major one, he was known as a theologian and his voice was respected. At first, he did not like the idea of the state passing laws to put down the Donatists, partly out of fear it would make martyrs who then would further the movement. This did happen, and the Donatists picked up several supporters who opposed state intervention in the life of the church. However, when the state did come in, Augustine saw that many people returned to the larger, catholic church, or came in for the first time, saying that they had been afraid to leave the Donatists before the state intervened. At this point Augustine changed his mind.

We need to remember the setting. The state was now officially Christian, and that only recently. States have certain obligations, among them protecting the population from invasion by others and keeping the public order within. Only a few generations earlier the church had refused to allow soldiers to be baptized because their duties conflicted with the ethics required of Christians, and since they were under orders of non-Christians, they could do little about it. What happens, however, when the state and all of its officers are part of the church? Can you have a pacifist state? Would this be permitting anarchy within its borders and easy invasion by enemies beyond? What should a Christian state do about such matters? We may raise questions as to the possibility of a Christian state, but that was the reality Augustine was dealing with, and he was attempting to create an ethic not only for individual Christians but for the governments that controlled their public lives. Pagans had said that Christians were poor citizens because their pacifist stance weakened the state. In response to this criticism, Augustine developed his "just war" theory, stating under what conditions a Christian state could use force. It dealt with the proper reasons for going to war, which included having been invaded, and the proper ways to conduct war, which involved protecting civilian populations and fighting only with other military units. In all cases, war was to be a last resort and conducted in such a way that love for enemies remained. In regard to the Donatists, the state could argue that the division in the church that they created had disturbed the internal peace of the empire in North Africa.

The second issue was whether official actions of the church—consecration of a bishop, ordination, baptism, Communion, and so forth—depended for their validity on the holiness of the person performing them. Augustine said no. If the proper person, in terms of office, using the proper words and elements, performs the ritual, it is valid, even if the person is flawed. In fact, what Augustine said was that the true minister, the true celebrant in any sacrament of the church, is Jesus himself, working through human ministers.

There is great strength in this position. To see that our baptism is an action of Jesus himself, welcoming us into the church, or an act of God, welcoming us into the family in which Jesus is the firstborn and we are adopted brothers

and sisters, makes this sacrament far more significant than seeing it merely as a human action. Understanding that in Communion it is the risen Jesus himself who invites us to the table and serves us the bread and cup is far more significant than viewing this simply as an action of the church. Here Augustine follows a far more ancient view.

There was another issue, closely related to this one. After the state had weakened the Donatists, at least to the point that they no longer threatened catholic Christians, many who had been baptized by the Donatists now wished to enter the larger church. Was their baptism valid, or, since they had been baptized in a schismatic church, should their baptism be considered null and void? Baptism in the Donatist churches used the same words and the same form as in the catholic congregations.

Earlier, after the persecutions in the middle of the third century, a famous bishop of Carthage, St. Cyprian, had to face the same question when there was another group that said the lapsed—that is, those who had sacrificed to the statue of the emperor—could never be reconciled to the church. This group was known as the Novatians. That schism did not last long, and when some who had been baptized by the Novatians wanted to join the catholic church, Cyprian had said they needed to be baptized again because they had not been baptized within the true church. Rome had disagreed with this position, but Cyprian said each bishop could do what he believed right in his own area. As he dealt with the issue, Augustine had Cyprian's words to consider. But he disagreed with Cyprian and said that as long as the Trinitarian formula and water were used, and the person performing the baptism intended to do what the church does, then the baptism was valid and should not be repeated. There should be a blessing, a laying on of hands, by the bishop to recognize that the person was now part of the universal church, but no new baptism should be performed.

In the case of an unworthy celebrant—in the situation that the Donatists first protested—or in the case of a schismatic baptism, the issue is the same. If the proper words and elements are used, and if what is done intends to be what the church does, then the ritual is valid and not to be repeated. But there are problems that lurk in this answer. We may be very glad that we do not have to have a full investigation of the life of the person who baptizes us or gives us Communion, but if the sacraments are somehow channels or means of grace, is grace a substance that we can automatically assume is received when proper rituals are performed?

It is precisely in the writings of Augustine against the Donatists that we begin to see grace not as a promise of God or as a relationship with God but as a substance that is automatically packaged with certain actions of the

church. This view would cause serious trouble later in the life of the church in the West. It was be a major issue at the Reformation. Is grace an encounter with God, an experience of God's presence in our lives, or is it more like a vitamin pill that does us good even if we feel nothing?

On the issue of the character of grace, Augustine's views, both positive and negative, show that he stands at the end of the early church, so that part of his theology reflects this older tradition, and he stands at the beginning of the medieval church, and he so articulates views that will be expanded in the centuries to come.

In response to the Donatists, Augustine dealt with a third issue. How pure must a church be? Granted that all of us are sinful to some degree, how sinful can ministers be before their unworthiness invalidates their actions? Augustine's answer was to say that no church can be sinless. In fact, it will not be until God's final judgment that the wheat and the tares (Matt. 13:29–30) will be separated. Any church that tries to eliminate everyone who is sinful will end up with no church at all, or else it will only deal with some sins—as did the Donatists—and ignore other equally important ones. Granted, a person who has committed a serious crime ought to be removed from office in the church, but there is no need to go back and say that all the baptisms he or she performed are now to be considered invalid.

In the history of the church there have been groups that tried to eliminate everyone who committed a sin, and not only the pastors. But this usually entails considering only specific actions, like putting incense in front of the statue of the emperor, or commiting adultery, or murdering someone. It usually does not cover attitudes, hateful speech, greed, and so forth unless they lead to actions such as murder or theft. No church is sinless, and it is very difficult to decide how sinful a person can be and still be part of the church. In the twelfth and thirteenth centuries some people believed only a poor church could be Christian, and they demanded that the church give up all of its property. Some of their critics called them "Donatists" for this view.

In the context of the Dontatist controversy, Augustine described the "visible" and "invisible" church. The visible church is the one that meets, that gathers on Sunday, that celebrates baptism and Communion. This is Christ's church, however flawed, and though it may be filled with people who are only there because of the social advantages it might bring, we are called to be part of the visible church. The invisible church is known only to God and is the church we affirm when we say that we believe in the "one, holy, catholic church." The two do not totally coincide. There are some in the visible church who are not in the invisible, but only God can sort that out. There are some who are in the invisible church who are not yet in the visible and may die before they are able to join it,

though the Holy Spirit is working in their lives. We are called to be part of the visible church and to be faithful to it. We cannot "join" the invisible church. At the point of the Reformation, both Luther and Calvin strongly held to Augustine's position on this point. Calvin in particular also believed the church had to be able to see that some members were excommunicated in order to keep the church's message clear, but the action of the church in no wise meant that the visible church could determine who was part of the invisible. That judgment had to be left with God.

The just war theory has undergone major challenges. Modern warfare does not make the distinction between military and civilian personnel. If a bomb is dropped, it probably kills more civilians than soldiers. Modern warfare is not carried out by armies physically opposing one another on a battlefield. There are also serious questions about preemptive attacks. In an age of air power, what does invasion mean? Above all, the question of being able to love one's enemies even while fighting them has proven futile. The first casualty of war often is the perceived humanity of the enemy. Hatred seems to be a necessary tool in modern warfare in order to mobilize the nation.

Augustine's view on baptism has continued to be the general stance of the Western churches, both Catholic and Protestant, with some notable exceptions. If a Presbyterian becomes a Methodist, he or she is not rebaptized. If a Roman Catholic becomes a Presbyterian, there is no rebaptism. If Presbyterians or Methodists or Lutherans become Roman Catholic, they are not rebaptized. However, if Unitarians or Quakers become Methodist or Roman Catholic, they are baptized, because there was no Trinitarian understanding (Unitarian) or no water (Quaker). Many other similar examples could be given. The great exception is those churches that do not hold to infant baptism. For them, baptism is a sign of the person's faith and therefore must come at an age when the person is able to confess to faith. And usually in these churches baptism must be by immersion. So if someone was baptized as an infant or not by immersion, a new baptism is probably required.

We are not accustomed to using the terms "visible" and "invisible" to describe the church today, although they can be very useful. The concept cuts two ways: it shows that no church can say it is both the visible and invisible church, that entrance into its fold guarantees salvation and that no other church is truly a church. The invisible church, the one, holy, catholic church, is not to be equated with any visible church or congregation, though hopefully there is considerable coincidence. On the other hand, we have a very different situation than Augustine faced. We have people today who believe they can be part of the invisible church without bothering with the visible—a view Augustine could not have imagined. In fact, such people may hold that the visible church, regardless of denomination, is simply filled with hypocrites, and they prefer to be part of "the church" without ever meeting with other Christians. Augustine's categories may be helpful in dealing with this situation, but it is not one that he considered. It was clear to him that from the human standpoint, there was no other way into the one, holy church of Christ than the visible church. God may have other means to bring human beings into the invisible church, but we do not.

Augustine's response to the Donatists elaborated a theology that still remains significant fifteen centuries after his work. We may view the theological results alone and find them useful. But it is helpful to see the social and cultural situations that produced them: the rise of a new emperor who supported the church, leaving Christians with new questions about how to live as the dominant religion rather than as a persecuted minority and the ethnic conflicts in North Africa, where Romans ruled the indigenous population. Such a background can give us greater understanding of the issues as even today, while living in an imperfect church, we struggle for its reformation and its purity.

CHAPTER EIGHT

Pelagius

Pelagianism is a defining issue in the whole Western church, both Roman Catholic and Protestant. No group in the Western church ever wants to be called Pelagian. Even those who disagree with Augustine's response to the Pelagians of his time go to great lengths to show that they themselves are not Pelagian.

How could such a negative view be held about a man whom even his greatest enemy—St. Augustine—rather liked?

Pelagius was born in the British Isles and raised there in the mid-fourth century. He was a devout Christian and took seriously the most rigorous demands of the Christian life. He believed in living simply, with humility and love for all. He was well educated, a layman, but really a reformer more than a theologian. That may have been his greatest weakness. He was in Rome in 405, and may have been there for two decades by that time, though when he left

Britain is unknown. In Rome he discovered that many Christians were quite unchanged from their previous, non-Christian lives. This was particularly true of the upper classes, many of whom had become Christians only after the church was clearly supported by the state. Pelagius was shocked at the lives of those who called themselves by the name of Christ. He urged them to improve their behavior. None of this would seem to be particularly dangerous to the church. Indeed, pastors and reformers have been urging Christians to live their faith since the church began.

Some responded well to his words. They agreed that the Christian life should be different from the traditional pattern of the old Roman Empire. When Pelagius was preaching the church had only recently expanded to include almost all of the population of the empire. The earlier requirement that those who wished to be baptized should spend two or three years as catechumens—students of the faith—before they were examined, to see if by their behavior as well as by their knowledge they were ready to become part of the church, was challenged. So many had asked to be baptized once the church was favored by the empire that the church simply could not train them. To refuse them baptism seemed a worse choice than letting them into the church and hoping to train them later. But Pelagius was appalled at the behavior he saw in the heart of the Western church, in Rome. Forgiveness seemed an easy matter without much repentance and change in lifestyle.

When people complained to Pelagius that they were only human and of course they sinned, Pelagius responded that the commandments were clear and that God would not have given them if we were not able to keep them. Surely it would have been unjust for God to ask us to do what was beyond our ability. If God commanded something, by definition it meant that we were able to do it.

Pelagius made it sound as if a human being could keep all of the commandments all of the time and therefore commit no sins. He never said he himself or any other that he knew was sinless—except for Jesus. But sinlessness was a human possibility, and we needed to put forth the effort to be sinless. He could quote Scripture: "Be perfect, therefore, as your heavenly Father is perfect" (Matt. 5:48). It was not only the Ten Commandments that he was considering. He believed that Jesus' instruction to the rich young man to sell all he had and give to the poor was also well within the realm of human possibility and should be done. Pelagius was disturbed by a prayer that Augustine wrote in his *Confessions*: "Give me what Thou enjoinest, and enjoin what Thou wilt." It sounded as though no effort was required on the part of the one praying and that all the work was up to God.

Pelagius left Rome in 409, just as the city was about to fall into the hands of Germanic invaders. He was in Carthage in 411. Though he and Augustine probably never met, both men wanted better behavior from Christians. Augustine's sermons show his forceful admonitions to his congregation. He recognized in Pelagius a devout

and humble man—a reformer. At this point in time, however, Augustine was so consumed with the Donatist controversy that he paid little attention to Pelagius's work.

If the matter had ended there, we would probably have heard little more about Pelagius. However, it soon became clear that Pelagius—and an increasing number of his followers—believed that all people are born with the same sinlessness as Adam before the fall. There is no sin until the person is of an age to be responsible for his or her own actions. For Augustine and others this raised the question of why infants were baptized if they were not sinful. This was the issue that set off the debate. Infant baptism was indeed the norm within the church, both East and West, and it had been for centuries. The children of those already baptized were usually baptized shortly after birth. In the case of adults coming into the church, if they had small children, the whole family was baptized. Before the church became so popular in the fourth century, one could assume that Christian parents would be sure their children were part of the church because the church was an unpopular group within the empire and its members clung to each other. But in the situation of the late fourth and early fifth centuries, that was no longer the case. Many of the parents whose children were baptized had minimal contact with the church, even though they were members.

By this time, within the West, baptism was understood mainly in terms of the forgiveness of sins. In the Eastern church and in the whole church before the third and fourth centuries, there were many other meanings of baptism: it was the engrafting of someone into the body of Christ, so that now he or she could be nurtured through Communion and the life of the church. It would make sense for an infant to be so grafted. But when the meaning of baptism was reduced to the forgiveness of sins, and then

114

one does not believe that infants and very young children are sinful, their baptism does not make sense. That was the challenge Pelagius faced. He agreed that infant baptism was good, but he seemed to make a distinction between infant and adult baptism, and that raised even more questions. If adult baptism is the sign of the forgiveness of past sins and the intention to lead a sinless life from then on, what happens when those baptized in infancy reach an age of accountability? Do they now need another baptism? As we saw with the Donatist controversy, the church at large was strongly opposed to second baptisms. Was Pelagius simply preaching another form of Donatism, now requiring adult commitment and perfect behavior after that?

Pelagius believed that though we were born with a clean slate in terms of sin, we are so surrounded by bad examples and have been ever since the fall that it is very difficult to

lead a sinless life. In fact, by the time we really want to try to be sinless, most of us have already committed sins. Pelagius believed that there was forgiveness for such past wrongdoings, and that Jesus gave us the perfect model in his own life so that we could choose to follow this model rather than that of the society around us. Pelagius also believed that there was forgiveness at the end of life but that it was somewhat dependent upon our really trying to be sinless now.

Pelagius did not stay in North Africa long but went into the Eastern areas of the church. He raised fewer questions there, for a variety of reasons—language among them. But a more radical disciple of Pelagius named Celestius came to North Africa, and many of his followers began preaching in various parts of the empire. At that point, people began raising questions about the theology that was behind these preachers' demands for reform. It was not long before many people appealed to Augustine to look into the matter and give his opinion.

Augustine's first concern was to preserve the necessity of baptism, especially for infants. For him, it was very clear that the major function of baptism was the forgiveness of sins. There was a long tradition in the church that all human beings were sinful. Paul constantly stresses that all of us have fallen short of the glory of God and that sinfulness is the human condition. Augustine agreed. But in what sense is an infant sinful? Augustine could readily use Paul's words about the first and second Adam (Rom. 5). If in Adam all sinned, does that mean that infants carry that sinfulness even at birth? Augustine answered yes, and developed a full understanding of what is called "original sin." He did not invent it, but he gave it a place in his theology that made the concept much more central and defined than it had been before.

Tertullian had believed that sin is inherited in the sense that sinful parents produce sinful children, in the same manner that blue-eyed parents produce blue-eyed children. However, Augustine did not agree with that view. Sinful parents do produce sinful children, but it is because in the very act of conception, "disordered passion," the mark of our fallen nature, is required. Here, Augustine's Neoplatonic philosophical inclinations are clear. Adam and Eve were created as fully adult, rational beings. This meant that the mind, the rational part of the human being, was completely in charge of the emotions, desires, and the body. There would be children, conceived in generally the same way as now, with the difference that there would be no passion, but simply a rational desire to have a child. The body of the man and woman would fully cooperate, and the sex act would lead to the birth of a child. No further sexual activity would be desired until it was rationally considered time to have another child. Obviously, in many ways, that scenario does not play after the fall. There is sexual desire when no child is wanted; there is no child conceived when it is desired; sexual passion and arousal are needed at least

on the part of the male. All of this represents "disordered passion," the body and the emotions out from under the proper control of the mind. It is in the midst of this "disordered passion" or concupiscence that children are conceived, and they bear the marks of their conception: they too are born with disordered passions. That means that every child is born with the mark of sin, even though the child has committed no sin of its own. This sin is "original" in two ways: it is the first sin, which is now passed on to all future generations, and it is the origin of all future sins in the individual. The child will grow up to be sinful because these disordered passions will be present before the first conscious act is completed. Baptism wipes away the guilt, but not the physical consequences, of original sin and of all personal sins committed up to that point. But if an infant dies unbaptized, then the guilt of this original sin is still with it, and it cannot enter God's presence.

Increasingly, and even long after Augustine's time, sins committed after baptism were dealt with by a new sacrament, penance, which involved confession to a priest. The absolution received put one back to baptismal purity. Therefore, all infants of Christian parents should be baptized as soon as possible after birth in order to ensure that they could enter the presence of God if they died before they were able to make an adult commitment.

According to Augustine, disordered passions are not only sexual, although that is important for the passing on of original sin. Every facet of our lives is disordered. This is what is meant by "total depravity." Even our minds are affected. What Augustine meant by total depravity is akin to what we today call "rationalization." Our minds are able to convince us that we are justified in taking a certain action usually considered sinful. Later, if we are able to reflect on the matter, we realize it was our self-interest, our greed, our desire for something that had clouded our judgment. We were, at the moment of choice, unable to think clearly and choose the right course of action. Total depravity does not mean that everything we do is completely wrong, but that everything we do is to some degree or another tainted by our own self-protectiveness.

Augustine then asked how God's work of redemption can come to human beings who are in such a state of total depravity. If we are presented with the gospel, wouldn't we simply evaluate it on the basis of our own disordered passions? We might decide it makes no sense and reject it because it would cost us too much. Or we might decide to accept it because it would bring us public approval. For Augustine, the only way we can truly see the gospel for what it is is through an act of God that overpowers our minds, that breaks through our self-protectiveness and makes us see what God is truly offering us. This overpowering act of God is what is called "irresistible grace." It is

grace, an action of God, but one that is so powerful it breaks through our defenses and makes us see what is true, both about ourselves and our sinfulness and about God and God's astonishing action in Jesus Christ. This irresistible grace begins the Christian life; we are thereafter, on occasion and increasingly, able to see the really good action. Grace begins to overcome the "total" of "total depravity." This does not mean that in this life we will cease to sin, but it does increase the sphere in which our free will can choose to do what is really good, and for good motives rather than self-serving ones.

Irresistible grace, however, implies that the experience of grace is one in which we feel we have been chosen by God rather than that we have chosen to believe. Belief is not something we can force ourselves to do. Rather, it is something we find ourselves doing. Irresistible grace leads to the doctrine of election: that God has given such irresistible grace to those whom God chooses, not based on what they have done or not done, and not on the basis of what God knows they will or will not do in the future. This is what is called "unconditional election," otherwise known as "predestination."

The final point is that if we did not choose to believe, if irresistible grace was given to us and therefore we believe, then we cannot cease believing of our own volition. This is what Augustine meant by "perseverance": those who have been elected by God to receive the grace that enables them to believe will persevere in their faith, even if there are pitfalls and valleys on the journey. Ultimately, their faith will be victorious over all their doubts and difficulties.

These are the terms for the four points of Augustine's writings against Pelagius: total depravity, irresistible grace, unconditional election, and perseverance. In the seventeenth century, in a revival of strict Augustinianism within the Dutch Reformed Church, a fifth one was added: limited atonement. We need not go into that here, except to say that neither Augustine nor Luther nor Calvin held to such a doctrine. With this added one, in English, the beginning letters of the five points spell the word TULIP, and this has been the mnemonic device for remembering this theological tradition. It remains a handy reminder of the main points of Augustine's writings against Pelagius, albeit without the L.

Augustine's theology clearly refutes Pelagius. Everything is due to the grace of God. Even our faith is the result of such grace. It makes sense of the prayer that Augustine wrote in his *Confessions*. However, his theology not only refutes Pelagius, but it raises several serious questions that troubled the church immediately after Augustine wrote and have continued to trouble the church in the centuries that have followed.

There is a clear connection between total depravity and irresistible grace. If our minds are so clouded by sin that we cannot see the gospel clearly, then we cannot choose it for what it is. Irresistible grace leads inexorably to the doctrine of election: that God chooses to give such grace to some and not to others. As a theological system, it is clear and coherent. There are many biblical passages that can be used to support it. However, it may have solved one problem—Pelagianism—only to create others.

Augustine's own understanding of election was even more limited than many later ones. He believed that, had there been no sin, only the proper number of human beings would have been born that was needed to replace the fallen angels. The excess human beings born are the result of the disordered passions due to the fall.

Augustine's view also seemed to minimize the need to proclaim the gospel, especially if the number of the elect was very limited. How does that square with the words of Jesus that we are to "make disciples of all nations" (Matt. 28:19)? There are also many biblical passages that proclaim God's desire for all to be saved. If that is so, why doesn't God give such irresistible grace to everyone? Augustine's limited number of redeemed soon was dropped, and the question of how many were elect was left as a mystery known only to God. But the relationship between preaching the gospel and irresistible grace remained unresolved. Later theologians who held to the doctrine of election agreed that irresistible grace operates at the point that a person is confronted with the proclamation of the gospel, and not independently of that proclamation. It is grace to open one's eyes to see the truth and beauty of the gospel that has been presented. Some people may be part of the church for a long time and have heard many sermons before the moment arrives when God's grace operates in their lives and they truly believe. Someone who is completely outside of the church may be brought by the power of the Holy Spirit into a place where he or she hears the gospel and is ready to believe. A doctrine of election does require that the gospel be preached in order that God's grace can do its work.

There is also the issue of sanctification. If one is convinced of being among the elect, does this mean that one can sin all one wants, because salvation is assured? Both Augustine and later theologians who agreed with him on election always responded no to this question. A sign of truly receiving the grace of God is a desire to follow the will of God as much as possible. Augustine did not believe Christians could have assurance that they were among the elect. They should rely on the church, its sacraments and its teaching, to give them the assurance that they were elect, that is, that they were part of the invisible as well as

the visible church—to use the terminology Augustine had developed in response to the Donatists.

The Pelagian controversy was the last major one to occupy Augustine's thought. He died shortly after these writings were complete. The Germanic tribe known as the Vandals broke through the walls of Hippo just after he died, and he was the last catholic bishop in Hippo. Many of his flock fled to Sicily and other areas, but the control of much of North Africa was now in the hands of the Vandals, who were Arian rather than catholic Christians.

There were many among the first readers of Augustine's anti-Pelagian writings who believed that he had undercut the nature of the Christian life. Some of them were monks in the south of what is today France, in monasteries around the present city of Marseilles. Why were they trying so hard to do God's will if it really did not matter and they might be damned after all? For them, God's grace was absolutely necessary; however, it was not an irresistible grace. It was resistible because the human mind was always able to see the good and choose it. We are all sinful, but it is because our wills are weak, not because our minds are corrupted. This group came to be called the "semi-Pelagians," though they could just as easily be called "semi-Augustinians." Because they insisted that grace was needed in order to strengthen the will and the desire to do God's will, they held that they were not Pelagian. We must cooperate with grace, but both grace and our active cooperation are needed in the journey of redemption. The technical terms that came from this debate are "monergism" and "synergism." In these words, the prefix *mono* means "one" and the prefix *syn* means "together." The *ergism* comes from the same root as "energy" and refers to work. In our salvation, is there one worker, which is God (monergism, Augustine's belief), or do God and the individual work together (synergism, the view of the semi-Pelagians)? Both positions are in agreement that Pelagius seemed to believe we really worked alone much of the time, except for the good example of Jesus. Both Augustine and his critics in southern France believed Jesus has to be a savior, a redeemer, and not simply a good example, a model, or a teacher, which was the major emphasis of Pelagius.

In the midst of those debates, a strong supporter of Augustine's position, Prosper of Aquitaine, summarized the problem of irresistible grace and election in these words:

> We must confess that God wills all men to be saved and to come to the knowledge of the truth. Secondly, there can be no doubt that all who actually come to the knowledge of the truth and to salvation, do so not in virtue of their own merits but of the efficacious help of divine grace. Thirdly, we must admit that human understanding is unable to fathom the depths

124

of God's judgements, and we ought not to inquire why He who wishes all men to be saved does not in fact save all. (*The Call of All Nations*, trans. P. De Letter, Ancient Christian Writers [New York: Newman Press, 1952], book 2, chap. 1)

That was not a very satisfactory conclusion, although it did state the problem clearly. It is no wonder that many opposed Augustine's solution and yet did not wish to deny that God's grace was essential to salvation.

After several debates, often conducted in the midst of further Germanic invasions, an agreement was reached in 529 at a synod in the French city of Orange. Since this was a debate only in the West, the synod dealing with it was a local council. Here we see an interesting compromise. We are born with total depravity, unable to choose the gospel of our own volition. However, at baptism (which is assumed to be shortly after birth), sufficient grace is given to allow us thereafter to choose by our own will. Grace is not irresistible, but it is necessary. There is no mention of those who are born outside the church, but probably there could be a bit of grace given to them as well, once they are

brought into contact with the gospel. Clearly this is not Pelagian, because grace is viewed as essential. Nor is it truly Augustinian, even though it was in this fashion that Augustine was bequeathed to the centuries that followed. We can see here the idea of grace as a substance, a thing, that is given in the sacraments and strengthens the ability to do God's will. Augustine was to some degree responsible for that, but the rest is not at all what he said.

Because of the lack of libraries and educational facilities, it was not until the ninth century that someone, a monk named Gottschalk, had the time and the inclination to read the anti-Pelagian writings of Augustine. He then wrote that what Augustine said was very different from what the church was teaching. He was condemned, and the issue remained dormant. St. Thomas Aquinas, writing in the thirteenth century, based his understanding of grace very much on the decision of the Synod of Orange.

It was not until the sixteenth century that Augustine's writings against Pelagius were again discovered. Both Luther and Calvin believed that the actual practice of the Roman Catholic Church in their day was Pelagian. The goal was to have sufficient merits, accrued by one's own actions, in order to enter at least purgatory if not heaven itself. (All those in purgatory would eventually enter heaven.) The Protestant reformers used Augustine's writings against Pelagius in order to refute those teachings. At the same time, these reformers also disagreed with the idea of grace as a thing, as a substance we receive through the sacraments of the church. In terms of election, Calvin in particular agreed with Augustine, though he also believed that through the action of the Holy Spirit we can be assured of our salvation.

The Roman Catholic Church also went through a reformation in the sixteenth century, culminating in the

Council of Trent. At that point, the theology of Thomas Aquinas became normative on the issue of grace. This was a return to the Synod of Orange, but with a strong emphasis on the need for grace. The more Pelagian elements that the Protestants rejected were eliminated. In fact, there were conflicts within the Catholic Church between those who were more like Thomas and those who were strongly Augustinian.

In the centuries after the Reformation, other denominations developed. John Wesley agreed far more with Thomas Aquinas than with Augustine, although without the idea of grace as a substance. The Baptists divided between those who held to election and irresistible grace, and those who held to free will and resistible grace in regard to salvation.

It is not only denominations that make a difference. Culture also plays its part. In the United States, we admire people who get ahead under their own power. No matter whether a denomination technically holds to a doctrine of election, our culture itself is inclined to Pelagianism, to the idea that our own work brings our reward. "God helps those who help themselves" is as much a part of our psyche as is the stress on the necessity of God's grace. In addition, many of our churches were strongly influenced by the revivals of the eighteenth and nineteenth centuries. Both the Methodists and the Baptists were born in these movements. The revival movement stressed that the future depends on our choice. That can be interpreted in a way that makes it quite Pelagian, or it can be nuanced to show the need for God's grace at every step.

The Western church has had to deal with the results of the Pelagian-Augustinian debate ever since the fifth century. We may well have overdefined the work of grace to make the various positions totally incompatible. But clear systems do not always mean accurate theology, whether it is Augustine, the Synod of Orange, or the various forms of Calvinism in later years. The work of God in our lives is a mystery, and we cannot define it fully. In fact, we are likely to understand our experience of grace in terms of the theological tradition in which we have been raised. At the same time, it is clear that God's grace is needed. However we understand it, we are fallen creatures, not simply good ones made in the image of God. In Christ, God has called us to a new life and made it possible through the death and resurrection of Jesus. We cannot do this by ourselves, nor are we asked to. The church, the body of Christ, is the context within which, in fear and trembling, we work out our salvation. It is the context also in which the grace of God finds us and nourishes us. The shadow of Pelagius still falls on the church. He was right that Christians should try to live out their convictions. He was wrong that the tempta-

tion to sin is only external, that it comes from the bad examples that surround us. The church holds that sin is within us. We need a savior. We need God's grace in our lives. Yet how that grace is given and does its work remains a mystery.

CHAPTER NINE

Christology

Who is this Jesus Christ whose importance is such that a worldwide religion is named after him? The question, which according to the Gospels Jesus himself was the first to pose to his disciples, has long been at the center of Christian life, worship, and theology. It has also led to bitter controversies and lasting divisions among Christians. The most notable of these controversies took place in the late fourth and early fifth centuries, becoming particularly bitter just after Augustine's death.

From a very early date, most Christians decided that some clear-cut extreme answers were not adequate. In chapter 2 we saw how for the Ebionites and other groups,

Jesus was mostly a unique human being, a faithful and obedient Jew whom God greatly exalted—or as some would say, adopted into sonship. While easily understood, this view did not adequately express the faith and the worship of most in the Christian community. The church did believe that Jesus was a faithful Jew, but it was also convinced that something radically new had happened in his life, death, and resurrection; that God was present in him in such a complete manner that it was legitimate to render him praise and worship without thereby falling into idolatry. For this reason the teaching of the Ebionites and others like them was soon discarded. Then, at the other extreme, there was the answer of the gnostics and other Docetists (see chapter 3). For them, Jesus was simply not human. There was no need for him to be, for he had not come to save whole human beings but only their eternal souls, entrapped as they were in material bodies. His unreal body was simply the means for him to convey his message from beyond. The church did believe that Jesus had brought a message from beyond, but it was also convinced that part of what was unique about Jesus was precisely that he was a human being like other human beings, with a true body and true physical needs—and above all that his death and resurrection were real, and not just some sham or sleight-of-hand perpetrated by God. Indeed, what came to be known as the Apostles' Creed, with its emphasis on the birth, suffering, death, and resurrection of Jesus, was formulated in part as a prescription against such views.

In brief, the church was convinced that Jesus was both truly human and truly divine. It was also convinced that Jesus is only one and not two different beings, one human and one divine. In this regard, it had rejected views such as that of Cerinthus (mentioned in chapter 3), who held that "Jesus" is the human being and "Christ" is the divine.

Thus, there were some clear limits as to what was acceptable and what was not. Ebionism on the one hand, and Docetism on the other, had both been declared to be out of bounds—and on this Christians generally agreed.

However, the haunting question remained: Who is this Jesus whom we love and follow, whom we are called to imitate as the best among us, and whom we are also called to worship as only God is worthy of adoration? This question, which every Christian throughout the ages has had to face, became the center of attention in a series of debates during the latter half of the fourth century and the first half of the fifth. These debates are usually called "the christological controversies," and their outcome set the framework for christological thought ever since and established further guidelines or limits that future orthodox theologians would follow.

In order to understand those controversies, we must see them both in their political and in their theological context. Politically, conditions had changed drastically during the fourth century. At the beginning of that century, the church was suffering the worst persecution of its history. Then Constantine decreed religious tolerance—and was eventually baptized on his deathbed. Constantine himself set a precedent by intervening in the Arian controversy. Most of his successors followed suit, to the point of trying to establish religious orthodoxy by imperial policy and fiat. The result was that questions of orthodoxy and heresy, which in the earlier church had to be settled by means of theological argument and persuasion, now could be settled by gaining political support from the state. This in turn meant that from this point on theological controversies would become nasty affairs. Those who lost imperial support could easily be deposed and exiled. Those who had such support did not often show much charity toward those who did not. Therefore, the history of developing christological orthodoxy is not pretty. In fact, it may well be the skeleton in the closet of Christian doctrine.

There were also issues of power and politics within the church. As we shall see in this chapter, the theological traditions of Antioch and Alexandria—particularly in matters having to do with Christology—were quite different. Since the West held the balance of power and was never as involved in the christological controversies as were Alexandria and Antioch, it was the West's more moderate tendencies, between Antioch and Alexandria, that eventually won the day. It was almost like a boxing match in which the two contenders are hurt and bloodied, while the referee, precisely because he is not involved, becomes more and more powerful as the match progresses.

Theologically, the debate around Arianism had set the

stage for the christological controversies. At Nicaea and Constantinople, the church had proclaimed that the one who is incarnate in Jesus—the second person of the Trinity—is fully divine, "of one substance" with God, the source of all things. From that point, an obvious next step in theological reflection would be to ask, How does this eternal, absolutely divine One relate to the humanity of Jesus? Or, simply stated, how can Jesus be a single, undivided being and yet be fully divine and fully human?

The greatest obstacle in responding to this question was that over the years the church had taken a theological route that would eventually lead to serious difficulties. In its earlier efforts to win converts from among the Greco-Roman intelligentsia, as well as to show that its doctrines were not as irrational and uncouth as its critics claimed, the church had tried to show the connection between its own monotheism and

the best of Greek philosophy. In order to do so, it had claimed that the one whom it called God was none other than the Supreme Being of which Plato, Aristotle, and others had spoken. This was a convincing argument and did much for the respectability of Christianity, although there are indications that the witness of believers to a life of love and faithfulness far beyond what their contemporaries considered reasonable did much more. The problem with the argument itself was that slowly but inexorably Christians began to think of their God in terms of the Supreme Being of philosophy. This was a being far removed from the materiality and transitoriness of all other beings. Furthermore, this being's uniqueness was often defined in terms of contrast with all things human, so that the divine attributes were defined either in terms of the lack of human limitations or by raising human abilities to the umpteenth degree. This becomes obvious as one looks at the following list of human and divine characteristics:

Humans are	God is
mutable	immutable
finite	infinite
passible (subject to the action of others)	impassible
mortal	immortal
temporal	eternal
limited in power	omnipotent
limited in knowledge	omniscient
limited in space	omnipresent

But then at the very core of the church's message was the conviction that God had become human! The church had simply painted itself into a corner. And it was a corner where long and acrimonious debates would take place.

The difficulty was something similar to what we would face were someone to ask us to produce a square baseball. By definition, a baseball is round. Also by definition, a square or a cube is not round. Our first response would probably be to simplify matters by eliminating one of the two horns of the dilemma. We might, for instance, take a baseball and subject it to a pressure such that it becomes a cube. In a sense, this was what the early adoptionists proposed: Jesus was a man, but his life was such that he became divine—he was adopted as God's Son. Problem solved!

However, as we saw in chapter 2, matters are not so simple. First of all, if Jesus is a mere man who has been adopted into sonship, it would seem that in worshiping him we are worshiping a mere creature, and thus falling into idolatry. Second, if Jesus was a man of such excellence that he became, so to speak, divine, this in itself robs him of his true humanity. A baseball shaped into a cube may be a baseball as far as its matter is concerned, but it is no

longer a baseball because it cannot function as a baseball. Just try playing with it!

There is another easy solution. Take the box in which a baseball was packaged, show it around, and claim that it is a baseball, even though the box is in fact empty. Jesus was truly divine. He was truly a being from on high. But as far as being human, this was mere appearance.

That was the solution of the Docetists, whom we encountered in chapter 3. But this is no solution at all. If Jesus merely seemed human, he was not truly human. He was not one of us. His life, his death, and his resurrection were all sham—a sort of show put on by God to make us think that these things were real, when in fact they were not.

By the time we come to the late fourth century, after the Trinitarian controversies discussed in chapter 6, most agreed that such easy solutions were wrong and that it was necessary to affirm Jesus as both divine and human. Essentially, this is what is meant by the doctrine of the incarnation—that, as John 1:14 says, the eternal Word of God became flesh and dwelt among us.

Given the way in which "divine" and "human" were defined, Christian thinkers sought to explain this in one of two ways. On the one hand, there were those who sought to safeguard the reality of the humanity of Christ by somehow making sure that this was not diminished by his divinity. Christologies of this type are usually called "disjunctive" Christologies, for they tend to disjoin the Savior's humanity from his divinity. This school of thought was particularly present in the region around the Holy Land, whose main city was Antioch, and therefore its Christology is usually called "Antiochene."

On the other hand, there were those who feared that the Antiochene position tended to divide the Savior in two, with a human being and a divine being. They insisted on the unity of the Savior, and their Christologies are commonly known as "unitive." Since Alexandria was the center for this school of thought, such Christologies are often called "Alexandrine."

Clearly, each of these two schools of thought was holding on to something important. The Alexandrines were right in affirming that Christ is only one and that he cannot be divided into two beings, one divine and the other human. The Antiochenes were right in rejecting any view that, while affirming the unity of the Savior, did this at the expense of his true humanity.

The debates were long and often bitter, and were made more so by the repeated intervention of imperial authorities.

One could say that the first round in the christological controversies revolved around the teachings of Apollinaris, a bishop of strong Alexandrine tendencies. Apollinaris simply suggested that the union of the divine and the human in Christ means that in him the eternal Word of God took the place of the "rational soul"—what today we could simply call "the mind." Jesus had a human body like any other human being, and this body lived as any other body lives. But instead of a human mind and soul he had the Word of God, the eternal Son. In the example of the square baseball, it was as if one took the core of a baseball and then wrapped around it a square leather casing. It is a ball. It has all the components of a ball. Yet it is a cube.

Apollinaris's suggestion was not well received. The main argument was that if the Word took on human nature in order to save humanity, he must have taken on precisely that part of a human being where sin is most powerful and where sin is conceived, namely, the mind. It is not just the body that needs redemption, but also the mind. As one theologian said, "What is not assumed is not saved"—with the consequence that if Apollinaris is

correct, Jesus can only save the human body but not the very seat of human sin.

Although these initial stages of the controversy were relatively mild when compared with later episodes, the result was that the Council of Constantinople, in 381, rejected the doctrines of Apollinaris, declaring them heretical because they denied the full humanity of Jesus.

So at the end of round 1 one could say that, although there were few telling blows, the decision went against Alexandrine Christology. Round 1 went to Antioch, with the support of Rome.

The next main stage in the controversy revolved around the person and teachings of Nestorius, a patriarch of Constantinople of clear Antiochene views. Constantinople was not one of the great ancient patriarchates—Rome, Alexandria, and Antioch—but it became a prize for which Alexandria and Antioch vied with each other. Each wanted to have its man on the see of Constantinople, which was the seat of imperial power. Thus, when Nestorius became patriarch of Constantinople, it was to be expected that Alexandria and its supporters would be looking for an opportunity to discredit him and perhaps even have him deposed.

That opportunity came when someone preached a sermon in which he declared that Mary should not be called "Mother of God" but rather "Mother of Christ." When people criticized the preacher, Nestorius came to his defense. Although the catchphrase referred to Mary, the debate was not really about Mary but about Jesus. Could one claim that God was born of Mary, or only that Christ was born of Mary? Could one claim that God walked in Galilee, or only Christ? Could one declare that God was crucified, or only Christ? In typically Antiochene fashion, Nestorius insisted that the divinity and the humanity of Christ have to be kept in clear distinction; if not, the divinity would overwhelm the humanity. The formula he used, which became the hallmark of Nestorianism, was that in Christ there are "two natures and two persons"—the divine and the human natures and persons.

His Alexandrine critics, as well as many moderate theologians, protested that this was tantamount to denying the incarnation of God in Jesus. It was like showing a baseball in its box and declaring that the ball is square because it is in a square box. Wherever the box goes, so does the ball, and whatever befalls the box also befalls the ball. The box and the ball are not really joined, even though they are not separate; they are two different realities, but as long as the ball remains in the box it is as if the two were one.

This second round in the christological bout was much nastier than the first. A council of the whole church was

convened to meet in Ephesus in 431. But the divisions and animosity were such that there were actually two councils running at practically the same time, with one representing those of Alexandrine tendencies and a smaller one taking the side of Nestorius and the Antiochenes. These two councils excommunicated each other, each declaring the other to be false. The emperor intervened, incarcerated the main leaders of both parties, and forced them to come to terms. Finally, a sort of truce was reached. The Alexandrines relinquished some of their more extreme demands, Nestorius's supporters agreed to a compromise, and Nestorius himself was declared a heretic and deposed. Thus, although the Antiochenes did land some punches, round 2 went to Alexandria—again, with the support of Rome.

The third round—the last one to be discussed here, although controversies and clashes between Antiochene and Alexandrine views continued for centuries—revolved around a monk named Eutyches. It was the middle of the fifth century. The imperial throne was occupied by Theodosius II, a weak and ineffectual ruler who left most decisions in the hands of the palace chamberlain. The patriarch of Constantinople, Flavian, was a fairly moderate defender of Antiochene theology. He had to confront the case of Eutyches, whose Alexandrine leanings led him to declare that in Jesus there was only one person and one nature. Although the details of what Eutyches actually said are not clear, it seems safe to say that at the very least he understood the incarnation in such a way that the divinity of the Savior eclipsed and even overwhelmed his humanity. (Some say that he held that the body of Jesus was of a heavenly substance, but this is not altogether certain.) He and his supporters held to the formula "one person and one nature" in Christ, for which reason they were dubbed "Monophysites," meaning proponents of a single nature. In our example of a square baseball, Eutyches apparently would have taken leather, cord, and all the other components of a baseball, made a cube out of them, and declared that this was indeed a square ball. The only problem was that it had never been a ball. Flavian declared these teachings to be wrong. Dioscorus, the patriarch of Alexandria, intervened in defense of Eutyches, who now became a mere pawn in a battle of giants. Alexandrine gold seems to have flowed into the hands of Theodosius's chamberlain. Finally, another great council was convened, and this gathered at Ephesus in 449.

This part of the fight was clearly rigged. The bishop of Rome, Pope Leo I, sent a theological letter taking an intermediate position between Alexandria and Antioch and declaring that Eutyches was wrong. Those running the council did not allow this letter to be read. When Flavian read his own confession of faith he was physically abused to such a point that he died a few days later. All bishops of Antiochene tendencies were declared heretical and deposed. Thus, the third round seems to have gone to Alexandria, by a definitive knockout.

In Rome, Leo cried foul. He appealed to Theodosius, but the emperor simply left matters in the hands of his chamberlain, who was clearly on the side of the Alexandrines. Leo declared that what had taken place in Ephesus was a *latrocinum*—a grand theft, or a robbers' synod. But all was to no avail.

Then the unexpected happened. Theodosius was out hunting when his horse stumbled, apparently in a gopher hole. The emperor fell and was killed. The throne then passed to his sister, Empress Pulcheria, who had long supported Leo in his protests. A new council was convened, and this met in the city of Chalcedon in 451. This Council of Chalcedon—now considered the Fourth Ecumenical Council by most churches—restored those who had been deposed by the "robbers' synod" two years before. After

much debate, this council produced a *Definition of Faith* that sought to navigate a middle ground between Antioch and Alexandria. In this regard, it affirmed the formula "two natures [the divine and the human] in a single person," which was very similar to other formulas that had appeared in the West over two hundred years earlier.

The Chalcedonian *Definition of Faith* is not a literary masterpiece. It certainly is not something one would repeat in church, like the Apostles' or the Nicene Creeds. In fact, at first reading it seems to be little more than double-talk and mumbo jumbo. It says, for instance, that Christ exists "in two natures, without confusion, without change, without division, without separation; the difference of the natures having been in no wise taken away by reason of the union . . ."

The purpose of such apparent double-talk becomes clearer when one remembers what was said earlier regarding the nature of doctrines. They are not so much descriptions of how things are as they are signposts or fences indicating where error and danger lie. In short, what was decided at Chalcedon was to reject both the Alexandrine and the Antiochene extremes. Against the former stood the phrase "in two natures"; against the latter, "in one person."

The Council of Chalcedon did not end the debate—no one could. Some rejected the single person that Chalcedon advocated, and came to be known as "Nestorians." Others, the Monophysites, rejected its insistence on two natures— the divine and the human. To this day, there are a number of Nestorian and Monophysite churches, particularly in the Near East. Many among the members of various churches unknowingly take positions very similar to one of the ancient heresies that this long process excluded. For instance, it is quite common to find those who believe that Jesus had no human mind and no human thoughts, that he was human only in his body. This is a modern-day version of Apollinarianism and presents all the difficulties of that doctrine. Even those who are aware of those ancient debates, and of the implications of one position or the other, find themselves more inclined either toward a "unitive" or toward a "disjunctive" theology. Among the Reformers, for instance, Luther leaned more in the direction of a unitive Christology, and Calvin did so in the opposite direction.

One could say, however, that there are other possibilities to be explored. What would happen, for instance, if we took a different point of departure than the traditional contrast between all things divine and all things human—if we decided that, rather than beginning by determining who and how God is and then trying to figure out how such a God could be human, we began by asking what we can say about God as revealed in Jesus Christ?

Such explorations might prove fruitful. We would no longer be engaged in trying to produce a square baseball. The christological debates of the fourth and fifth centuries would then be seen as based to a large extent on mistaken premises. But still, the signposts and fences resulting from those debates would prove valuable for our generation as well as for future ones. Once again, those who were eventually declared heretical have made an enormous contribution to Christian theology and faith.

CHAPTER TEN

What Now?

Our journey has been long, at times informative, at times exhilarating, at times bewildering, and probably at times boring! We have quickly surveyed four centuries of Christian thought and doctrine. In the process, we have come across strange names and doctrines—Marcion, Pelagius, Eutyches, Gnosticism, and others. Many of them may seem alien to us, but others strangely familiar. In the process, we seem to have desacralized much of Christian doctrine. It clearly did not fall from heaven. It clearly was not revealed to some mystic whom God chose as a mouthpiece. It is not even a summary of the belief of early Christians! It is the result of a combination of factors, all interwoven, and whose relative importance is not easy to assess. In many cases it developed as an attempt to express in more logical

fashion what the church was repeatedly confessing and proclaiming in its worship and in its witness. It is also to a large
degree the result of the love of God on the part of people
whose very love leads them to inquire more, to explore
possibilities, to suggest the unexpected. It often developed
as the reaction of others of opposite mien who believed
that more inquiry would only lead to unfaith, that the
promises offered by new possibilities and unexpected
developments would fall far short of the dangers they
entail. But that is not all. There was the constant presence
of power struggles within the church, and different views
as to the church's mission in a particular setting. There was
also the intervention of emperors and politicians who convened councils, deposed and exiled bishops and theologians, and in general thought that their civil power gave
them a particular role in matters theological. And there was
Theodosius's horse!

If we needed any proof that doctrine does not fall down
from heaven, Theodosius's horse should suffice. The
annulment of the decision of the "robbers' synod" of 449,
the convening of the Council of Chalcedon, and in general
all orthodox christological statements since then are in
debt to Theodosius's horse (or perhaps to the gopher that
dug the hole in which the horse stumbled). In order to
insist that doctrinal development is guided by God in such
a way that we can guarantee it is absolutely correct, one
would have to claim that God determined that Pulcheria
should reign, that Theodosius should fall and die, that the
horse should stumble, and that the gopher should dig. This
is a bit much to expect of even the staunchest believers in
divine Providence.

This being the case, what are we to do with all these
doctrines that developed out of struggles with heresy and
that clearly go beyond the New Testament? Are we to say

150

simply that all this doctrinal development is wrong and unwarranted and that all we are to do is return to the "simple" teachings of the New Testament? Some believe this. But then, when one looks into the matter more carefully, it is clear that the teachings of the New Testament are not all that "simple," and that in many ways doctrinal formulations that cannot be found in the New Testament help us understand the New Testament itself. Are we to claim that the Spirit of God made the church infallible, so that every doctrinal statement is fully authoritative, cannot be questioned, and is part of God's revealed truth? Some claim this. But then, it suffices to look at history to provide ample truth of the fallibility of the church. While doing much good and proclaiming much truth, at times the church has also insisted that the sun revolves around the earth, and that monarchy is an institution of divine and unquestioned authority. And then, of course, there is

151

Theodosius's horse. Thus, neither a "simple" return to the New Testament nor an absolute reliance on the authority of the church will help us out of this quandary.

Doctrines evolve—for instance, what many orthodox Christians before the time of Arius said about God and about Jesus is now considered heretical by most Christian churches, and what many before the time of Pelagius said about human capabilities is now rejected by most churches. Thus, the answer to our dilemma must be found along the lines of determining how it is that doctrines evolve and to what extent they remain faithful—or not—to the original message.

Perhaps the best metaphor to understand how it is possible for doctrine to evolve and yet remain true is to compare the development of doctrines with our own development. None of us is exactly the same as we were twenty or thirty years ago. When we look at pictures from our childhood sometimes we hardly recognize ourselves, yet we know that we are the same person. We are not the same, yet we are the same.

Let us look more closely at this metaphor. As in the case of doctrines, we cannot say that in order to be ourselves once again what we have to do is to return to our "simple" childhood. Many of us may want to do that. Those of us who are showing the wear and tear of age might dream of returning to the days of our youth. But the fact is that we cannot. We cannot, not only because it is impossible to reverse time, but also because the very passage of time has helped determine who we are. We are that child, yes, but we are also the young person who chose a career, the one who chose a mate, the one who had children, the one who has undergone a myriad of experiences that have made us who we are. Think of people going to a fiftieth high school reunion. They have changed so much that they have to wear name tags, because otherwise their classmates might no longer recognize them. Then, as they gather, one hears again and again, "My, you haven't changed a bit!" Obviously, there is an important measure of tact and diplomacy in such a remark, but there is also much truth. Once you begin talking with that classmate whose face you could hardly recognize, you rapidly become aware that you are dealing with the same person; that in spite of pot bellies, white hair, and wrinkles, the person with whom you are speaking is the same one with whom you went to a dance half a century ago.

At that point, our first reaction is to try to go back to those times, to act as if nothing had happened to either of us during the intervening decades. But we soon discover that this is impossible. The person before us, who "hasn't changed a bit," has indeed changed. Our old classmates have had experiences that have shaped who they are. The beauty queen may have gone through so many divorces and so many face lifts that she now looks tired and worn far beyond her years. The star quarterback may have succeeded at becoming a professional player, and that too has marked him. The quiet, unassuming girl nobody noticed may now be a worldwide authority in her chosen field of interest. We cannot erase any of that. If we are to relate with one another once again, we must relate as who we have become, as who we are now, and not as who we were fifty years ago.

To try to relate to our classmates as we did fifty years ago would be similar to trying to return to the "simple" New

Testament as if it has not been read, debated, explained, applied, and lived for almost twenty centuries. The message of the gospel has come to us through those twenty centuries—through good, bad, and in-between—and we cannot undo that history.

What we and our classmates have become is a combination of what was in our genes, the experiences we have had, and the decisions we have made. Likewise, what has happened to Christian doctrine as it develops is a combination of the original gospel message with the experiences and decisions of Christians through twenty centuries of proclaiming that message, of deciding how it is to be proclaimed, understood, and translated into different circumstances and cultures. In that process, as in the life of each one of us, there have been bad decisions. These have to be reversed, but they cannot be undone. If I spent five years pursuing the wrong career, I can now begin a new one, but I cannot recover those five years. What I can do is look at my decisions and their consequences in the light of who I know I am and should be, and then try to make the decisions and follow the paths that will make me more true to myself. Likewise, in the course of its history, when confronted with various issues, the church has made good and bad decisions. This is part of what the church has become; we cannot simply undo it. But we can try to reverse it, to correct it in the light of what the church is and what it is called to be—in other words, in the light of scriptural revelation.

This describes fairly accurately the manner in which doctrine has evolved and what should be our attitude toward such evolution. Faced by various challenges, the church has responded, and the result is the evolution of doctrine. Among those challenges, heresies—that is, doctrines that the church considered deviant—are foremost. Much doctrinal development has taken place as a response

to heresies, just as our decisions have taken place as a response to various suggestions, possibilities, and difficulties. Marcion claimed that the Hebrew Scriptures were the word of an alien, inferior god and suggested a new set of purely Christian Scriptures, with no connection with Judaism. The church responded by reaffirming the Hebrew Scriptures and developing its own list of New Testament books, all connected with the religion of Israel. Arius suggested that the one incarnate in Jesus is an inferior, secondary being, and the church responded by developing the Nicene Creed and the Trinitarian doctrine associated with it. The Donatists insisted that in order to be true the church had to be absolutely pure, and the church responded by developing a view of the Christian community as a body of sinners redeemed by Christ and constantly needing repentance and forgiveness.

However, the mere fact that the church made these decisions does not make them correct. The church also decided to condemn Galileo, and that clearly was not correct. The doctrinal decisions that the church has made in response to perceived heresy have to be judged again and again, always by the measure of Scripture, and always remembering that all such judgments are human and therefore fallible.

When, in that fiftieth reunion, we look back at our lives, there are decisions we wish we had not made, and there are others in which we rejoice. In general, however, if we have been wise we will discover that whatever bad decisions we made in our earliest days have been significantly corrected by later decisions, and that the good decisions still stand. The same is true when today we look back at the development of doctrine. There was a time in the second century when many Christians opted for Marcionism or for Gnosticism. Others decided against such options. What shows that the latter were right is the later history of Christianity, when Christians have repeatedly reaffirmed the early decisions against Gnosticism and Marcionism. There was a time immediately before the Council of Chalcedon when it appeared that Monophysism was to be the doctrine of the church. Then came Theodosius's horse and the Council of Chalcedon, and Monophysism was eventually rejected. But although officially it was the Council of Chalcedon that determined what orthodox Christology was to be, what in fact happened is that through a long series of debates and

alternative proposals most Christians came to the conclusion that Chalcedon was right—or at least more adequate than Monophysism. Thus, Theodosius's horse in fact played a very minor role in the final outcome—and, surprisingly, almost the same is true of the Council of Chalcedon, whose decisions were not immediately accepted by all. The major role in the entire controversy was played by countless worshiping believers who came to the conclusion that the decisions of Chalcedon best reflected the reality of this Jesus who was at the center of their worship.

We may find all of this disturbing. We may wish we could claim that our doctrines are exactly the same as the doctrines of the early church. But we cannot. All we can and must do is see ourselves as heirs to the great cloud of witnesses who struggled with the meaning of Christian truth and whose struggles are reflected in our present doctrines. We can take those doctrines as guidelines or signposts in today's struggles, so as not to fall into the same errors of earlier heretics.

Finally, we must remember that most of the heretics discussed in this book were not bad people. They were not trying to invent new doctrine simply to cause a disturbance. They were people whose love of God and of the Christian faith led them to inquire into a number of issues and to propose answers and solutions that the church at large found inadequate. Furthermore, they were not entirely wrong. Indeed, most of them affirmed an important truth that Christians should not forget. Thus, Marcion reminded the church that something radically new had taken place in Jesus of Nazareth; the Ebionites correctly insisted on the true and full humanity of Jesus; the Monophysites, on his true and full divinity. In a sense they were all partially right. More exactly, the most common problem with the ancient heretics was not that they were wrong, but that they were, so to speak, too right: they stressed an important truth so far that it led them to deny other important truths.

Perhaps this is the greatest lesson we can derive from the

history of Christian heresies: being too right is the first sign of heresy! This is certainly an urgent point to remember in our day, when so many of us run the risk not so much of being outright wrong, but of being too right.

For Further Reading

Since in a way this book covers much of the development of Christian thought and theology during the first four centuries, any of the standard church histories or histories of Christian thought would be helpful. The magazine *Christian History* has devoted an issue to "Heresy in the Early Church": issue 51, 1996. Justo has written a brief review that may serve as the next step in learning about the heretics discussed here, their impact, and the church's response: Justo L. González, *A Concise History of Christian Doctrine* (Nashville: Abingdon, 2005).

On the specific theme of the Ebionites, the following article, although rather technical, provides both helpful information and further bibliography: Richard Bauckham, "The Origin of the Ebionites," in *The Image of Judaeo-Christians in Ancient Christian and Jewish Literature*, ed. Peter J. Thomson and Doris Lambers-Petry (Tübingen: Mohr Siebeck, 2003), 162–181. There has been much written about Gnosticism in recent years. The most readily accessible material, providing connections and comparisons between ancient Gnosticism and its various recent revivals, is the fall 2007 issue of *Christian History*, which is devoted to this subject (Issue 96, 2007). A classic study on Marcion is E. C. Blackman, *Marcion and His Influence* (London: SPCK, 1948). On the manner in which the Apostles' Creed reflects a reaction to Marcionism, see Justo L. González, *The Apostles' Creed for Today* (Louisville, KY: Westminster John Knox Press, 2006).

For Further Reading

On Montanism, there are insightful pages in Jaroslav Pelikan, *The Christian Tradition: A History of the Development of Doctrine*, vol. 1 (Chicago: University of Chicago Press, 1971), 97–108. An older and much simpler treatment may be found in Robert M. Grant, *Second-Century Christianity: A Collection of Fragments* (London: SPCK, 1946), 94–108. The development and significance of the doctrine of the Trinity, and the impact of Arianism on it, has produced hundreds of volumes. The same is true of Christology. On both of these, consult Justo's *A Concise History of Christian Doctrine*. A much fuller treatment of the same subjects may be found in Justo L. González, *A History of Christian Thought*, vol. 1, rev. ed. (Nashville: Abingdon, 1987). There are fairly extensive discussions in J. N. D. Kelly, *Early Christian Doctrines* (New York: Harper & Brothers, 1960), 223–79 (on the Trinity), 280–374 (on Christology).

Much can be found on both Donatism and Pelagianism in any of the many introductions to the theology of St. Augustine. Look, for instance, at Gerald Bonner, *St. Augustine of Hippo: Life and Controversies* (London: SCM Press, 1963), which has extensive sections on both Donatism and Pelagianism. On Donatism, consult W. H. C. Frend, *The Donatist Church: A Movement of Protest in Roman North Africa* (Oxford: Clarendon, 1952). This is a classical study of the Donatist movement that takes into account the social and cultural conflicts of the time. A good introduction to Pelagianism is John Ferguson, *Pelagius* (Cambridge: W. Heffer & Sons, 1956).

Index

Index

Index

Sabbath, 17
Sabellianism, 25,
    80–82
Sabellius, 80–82
sacraments, 54
    validity of, 103–5,
    106
sacrifices, 17–18, 19,
    21, 59
salvation, 34–35, 41,
    43
sanctification, 56,
    122
Scofield, Cyrus, 75
*Scofield Reference
    Bible*, 75
semi-Pelagians, 124
Simon of Cyrene, 38
sinlessness, 114
sin
    after baptism,
        55–56, 57
    forgiveness of, 55,
        69, 98, 116
    original, 116–18

Socinianism, 27–28
Sophia, 23, 92
speaking in tongues,
    65
substance, 83, 88,
    135. *See also* Trin-
    ity; *homoousios*
synergism, 124

Temple worship,
    17–18
Tertullian, 33, 43,
    55–56, 57,
    66–67, 69, 73,
    81–83, 89, 117
Tertullianists, 73
Theodosius II, 143,
    144
Thomas Aquinas,
    126, 127
traditores, 98
transcendentalism, 41
Trent, Council of, 127
Trinity, 57, 66,
    77–92, 135

gender and lan-
    guage regard-
    ing, 91–92
social implications
    of, 90–91, 92
Trypho, 23

Unitarianism, 26–27,
    90

Valentinians, 11
virgin birth, 18, 21,
    25
Vulgate, 3

Wesley, John, 127
women, 63–64, 67,
    70–71, 74
worship, 40, 46
    and theology, 8,
        78–80, 83, 84,
        86–87, 91,
        132, 133, 137,
        150, 158